I want to thank my parents for believing in me.
To my husband Michael for filling my head full of dreams
and a special thanks to my brother Clayton for helping me finalize my book
so I could share it with the world.

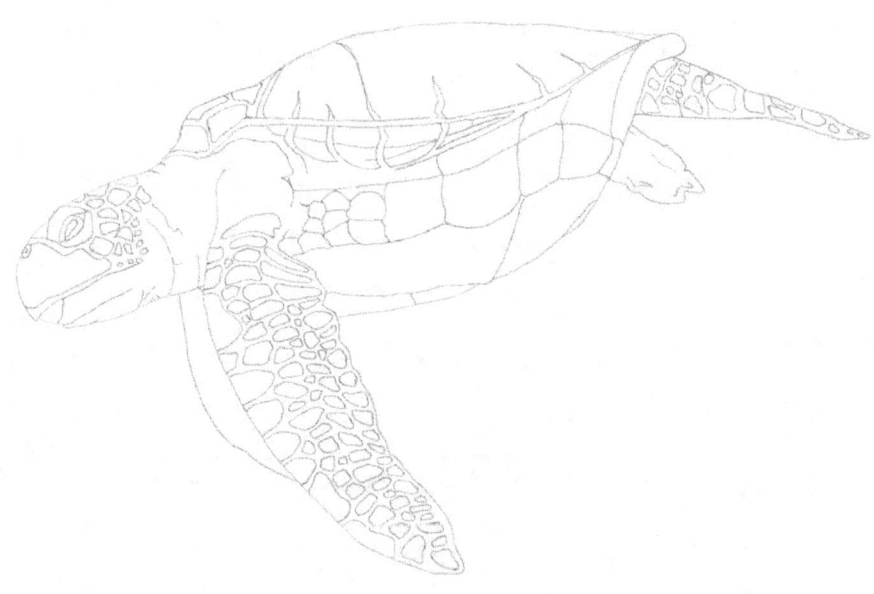

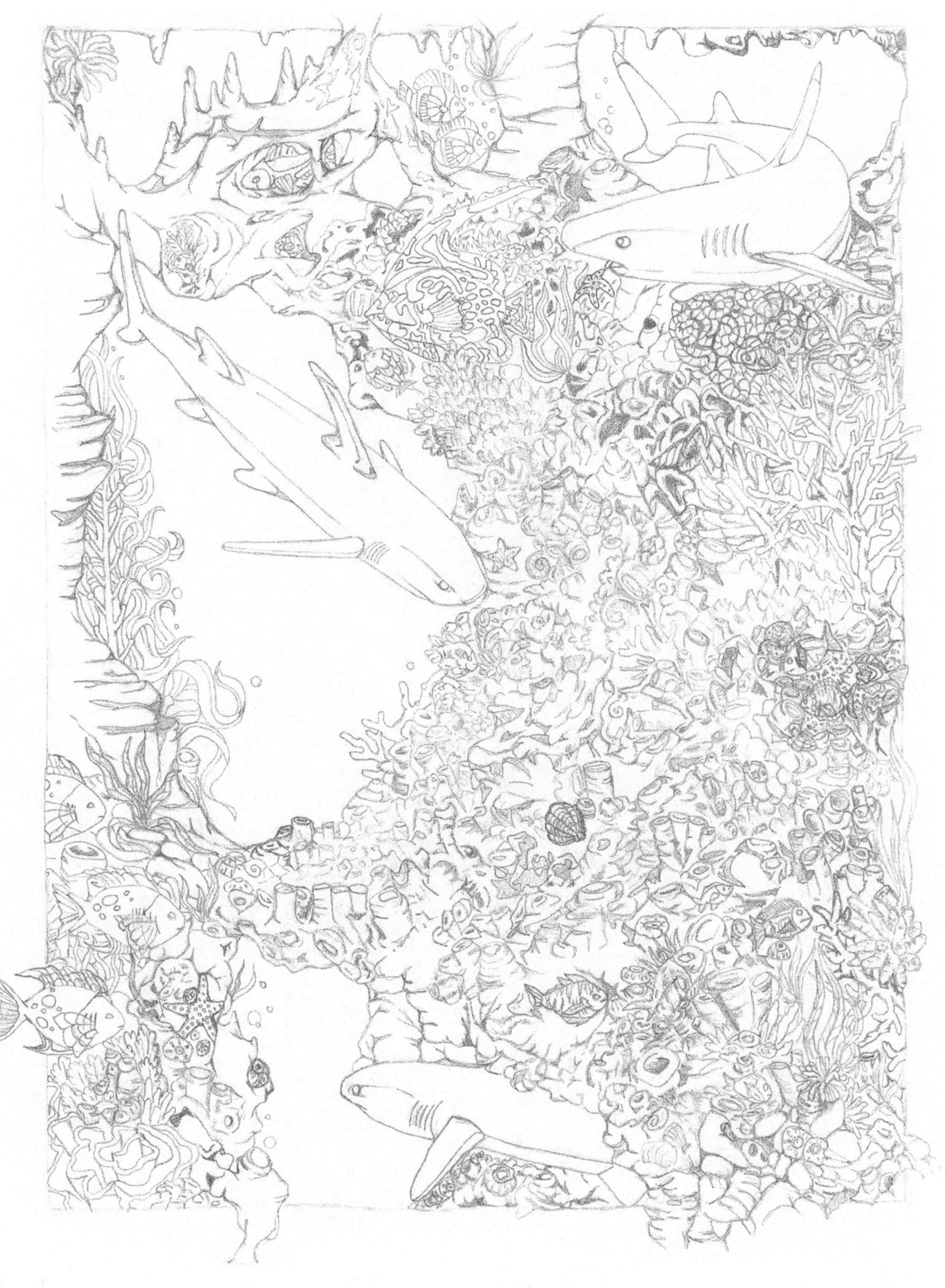

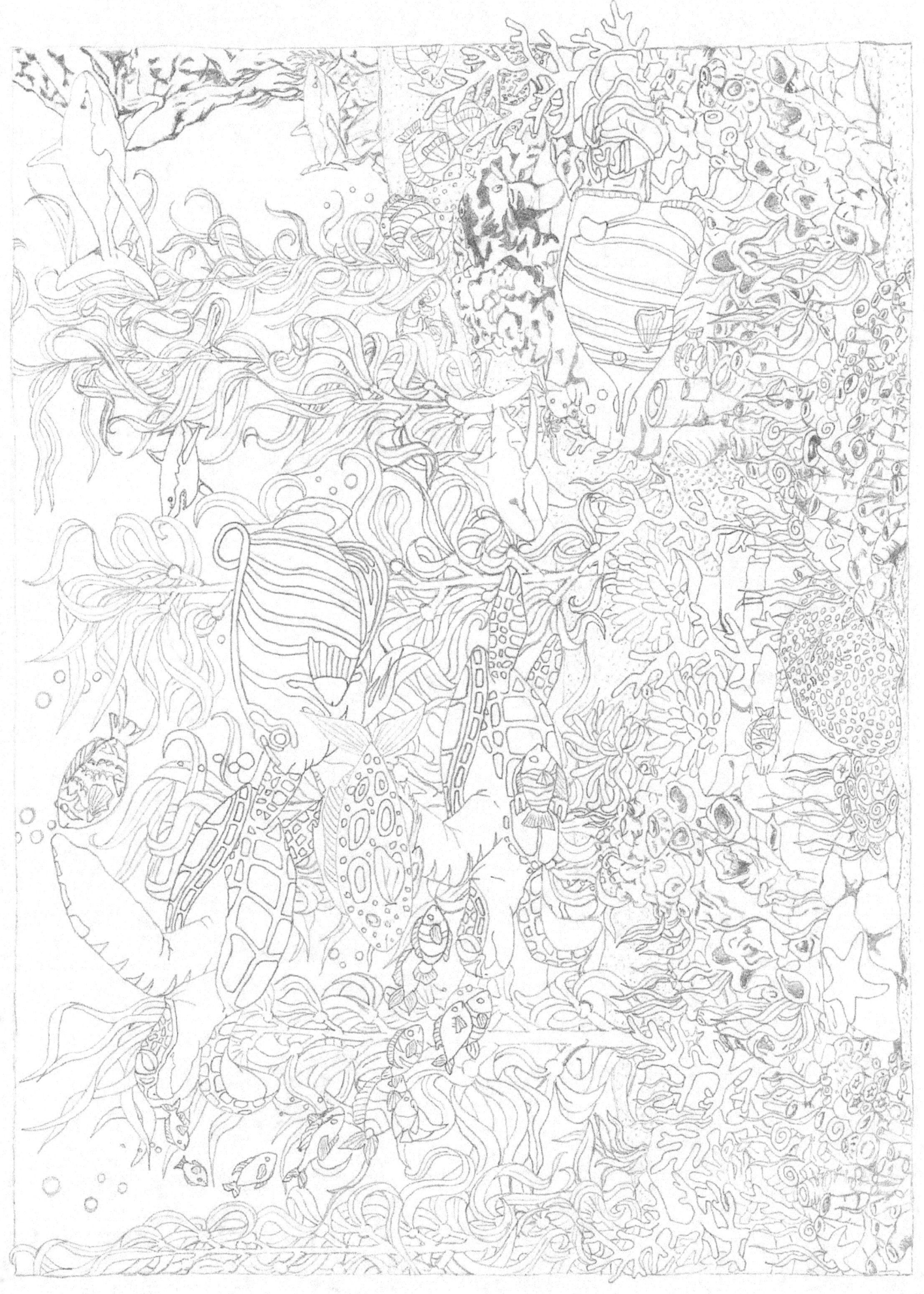

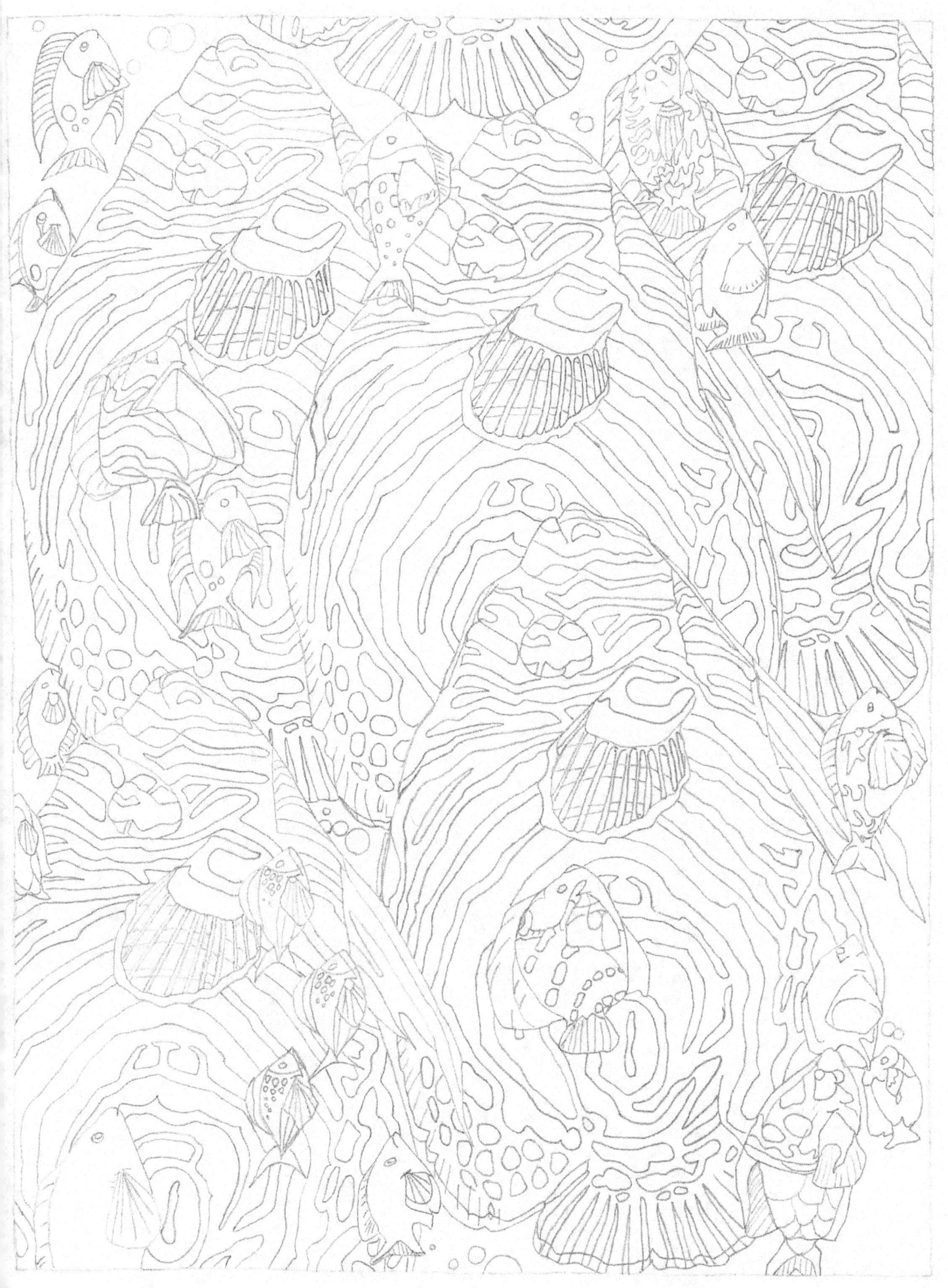

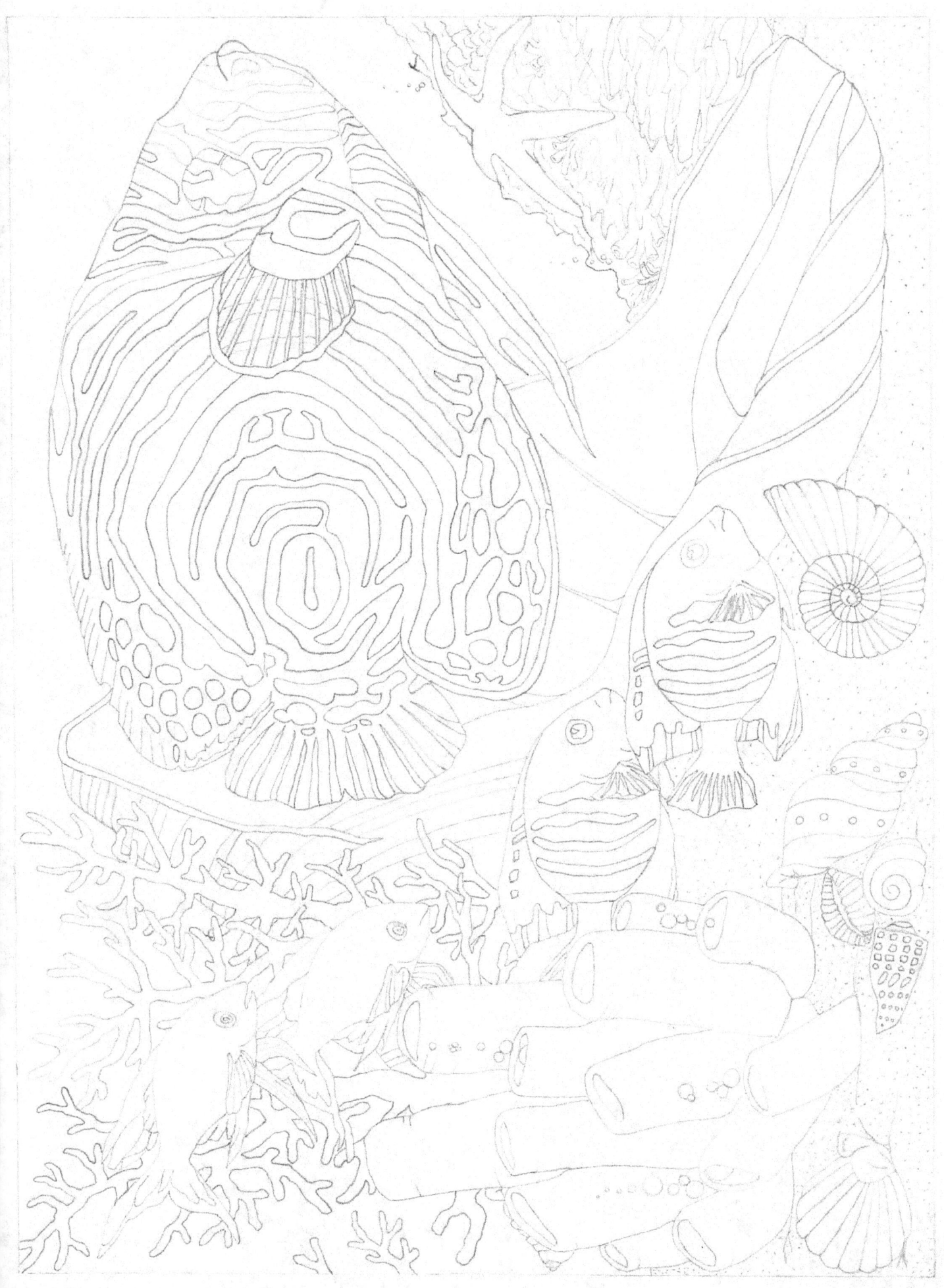

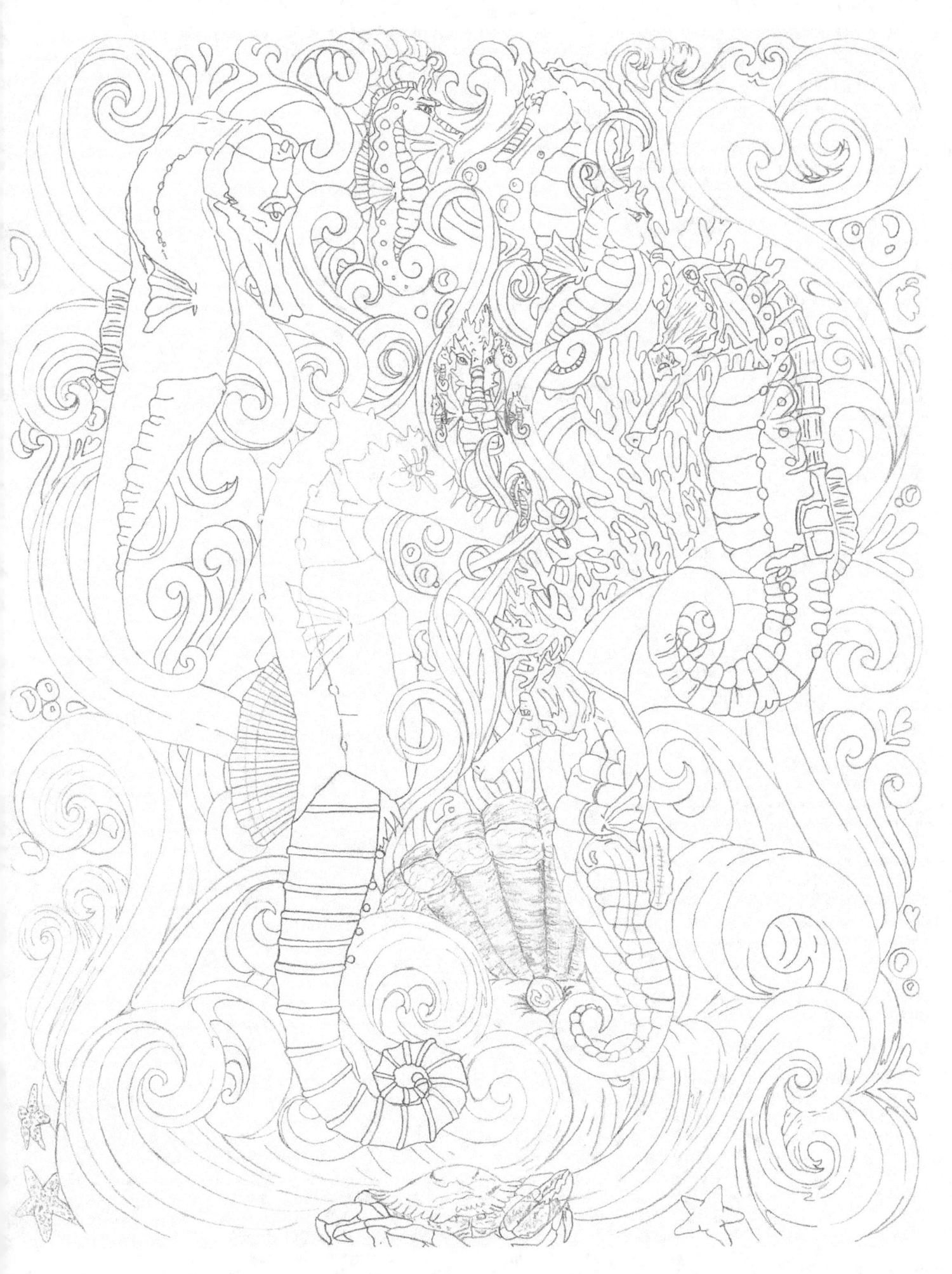

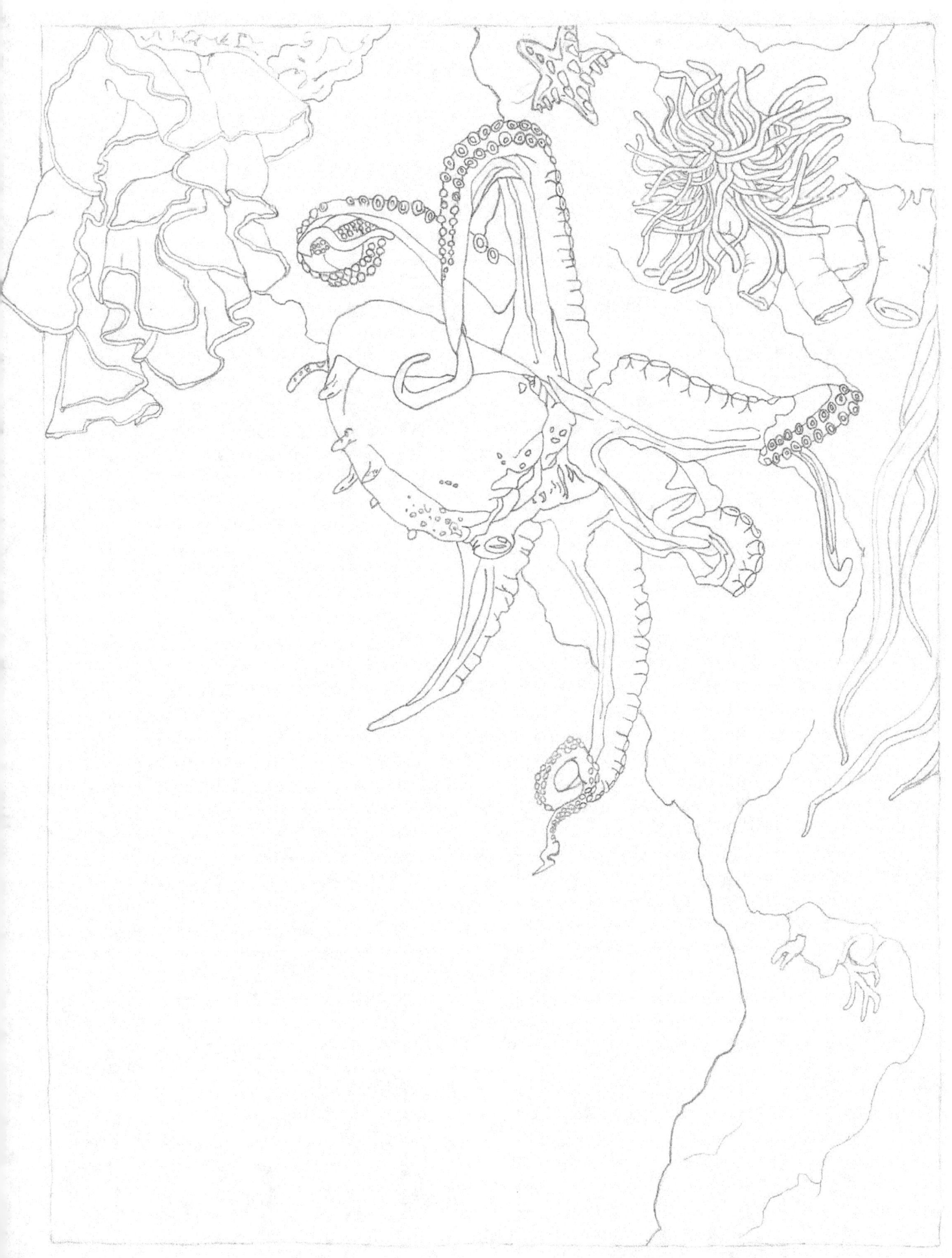

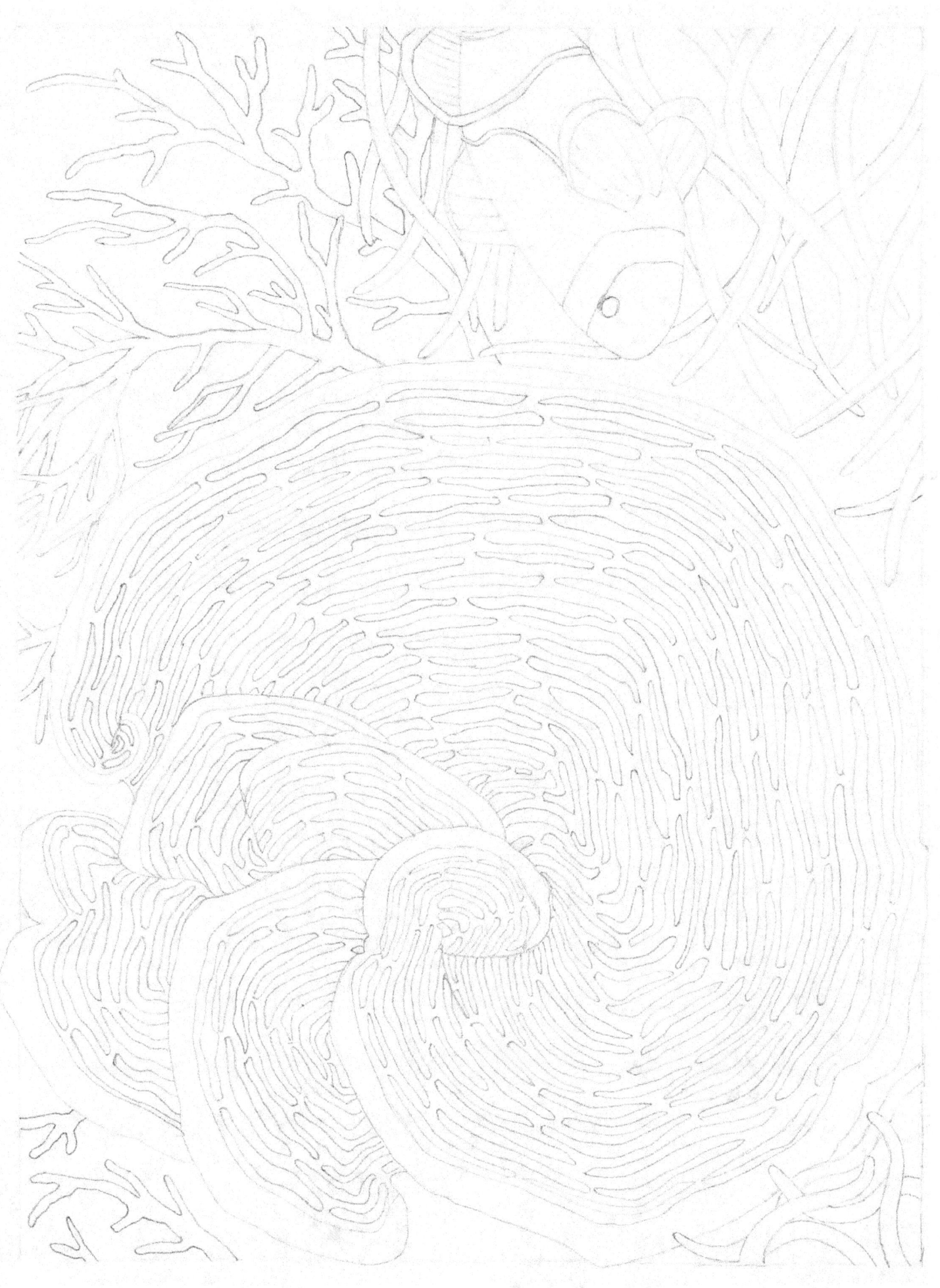

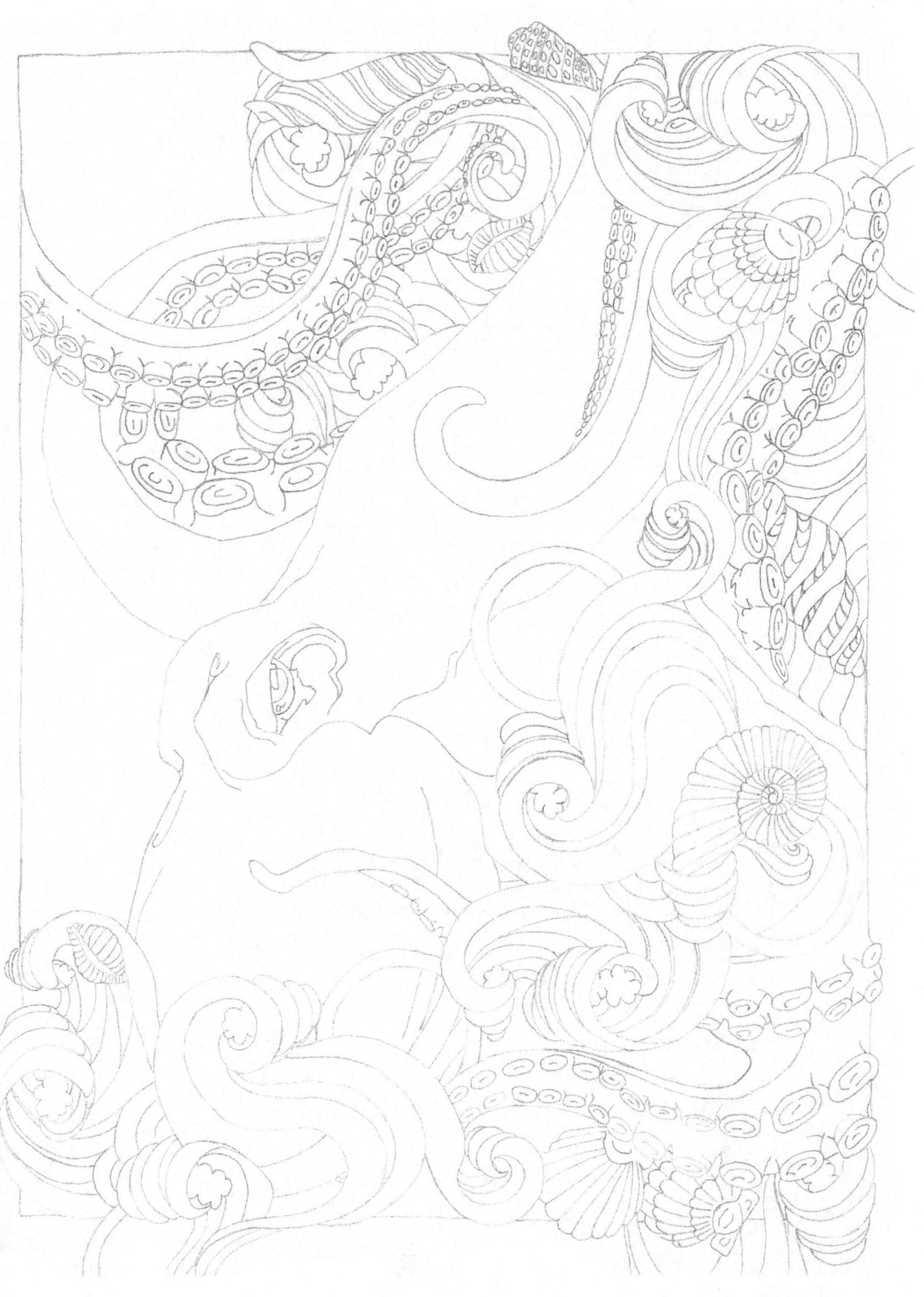

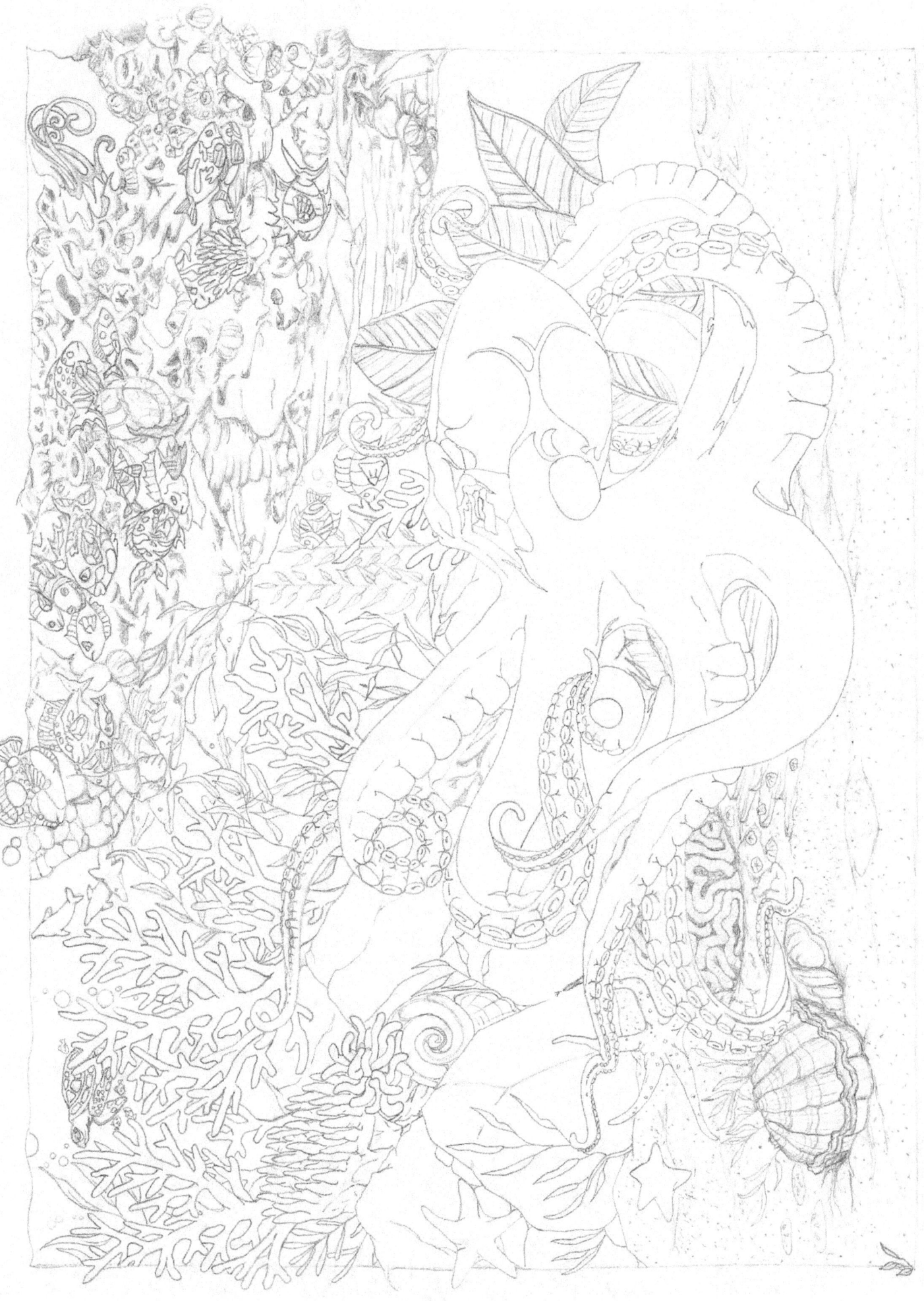

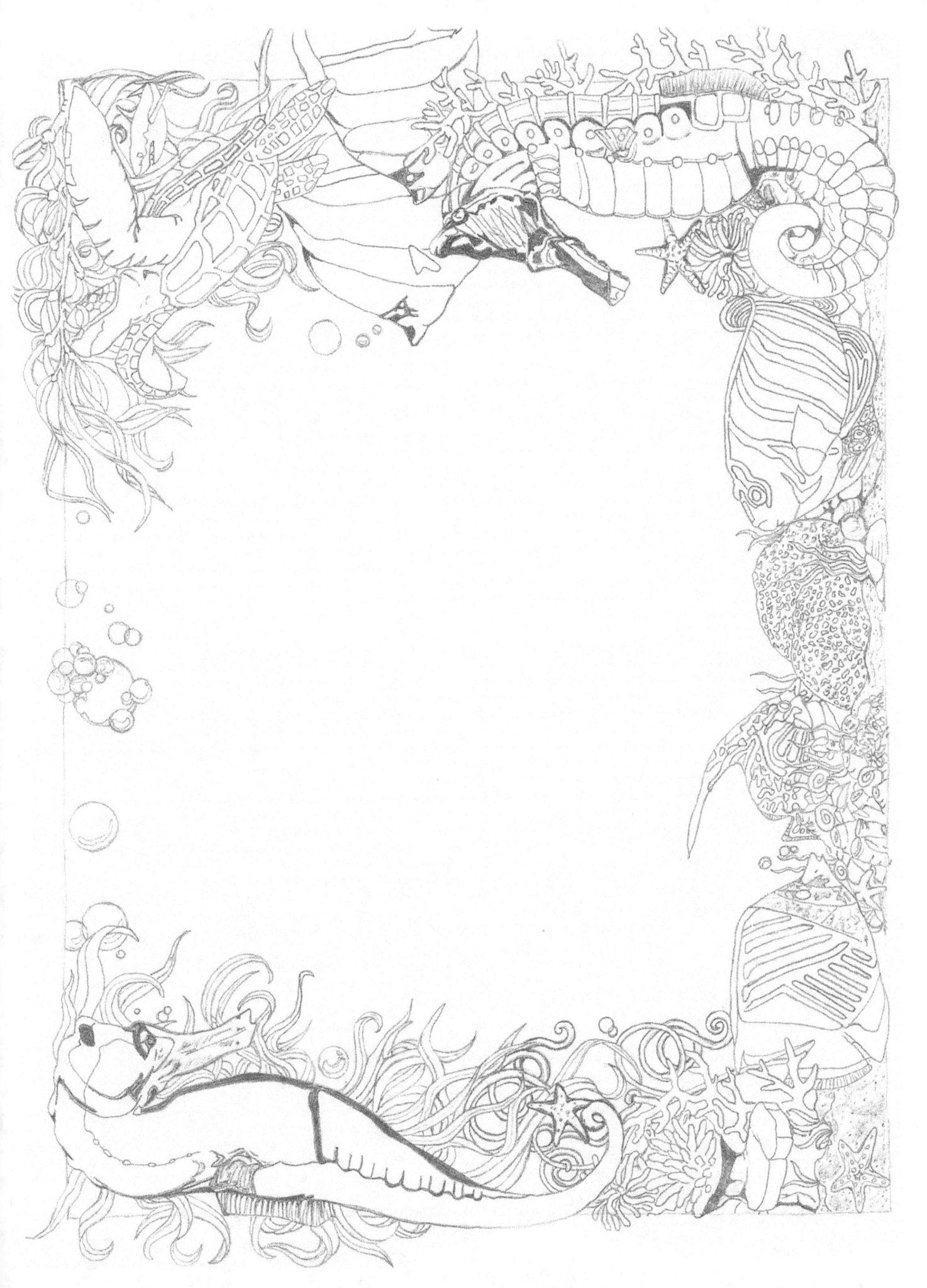

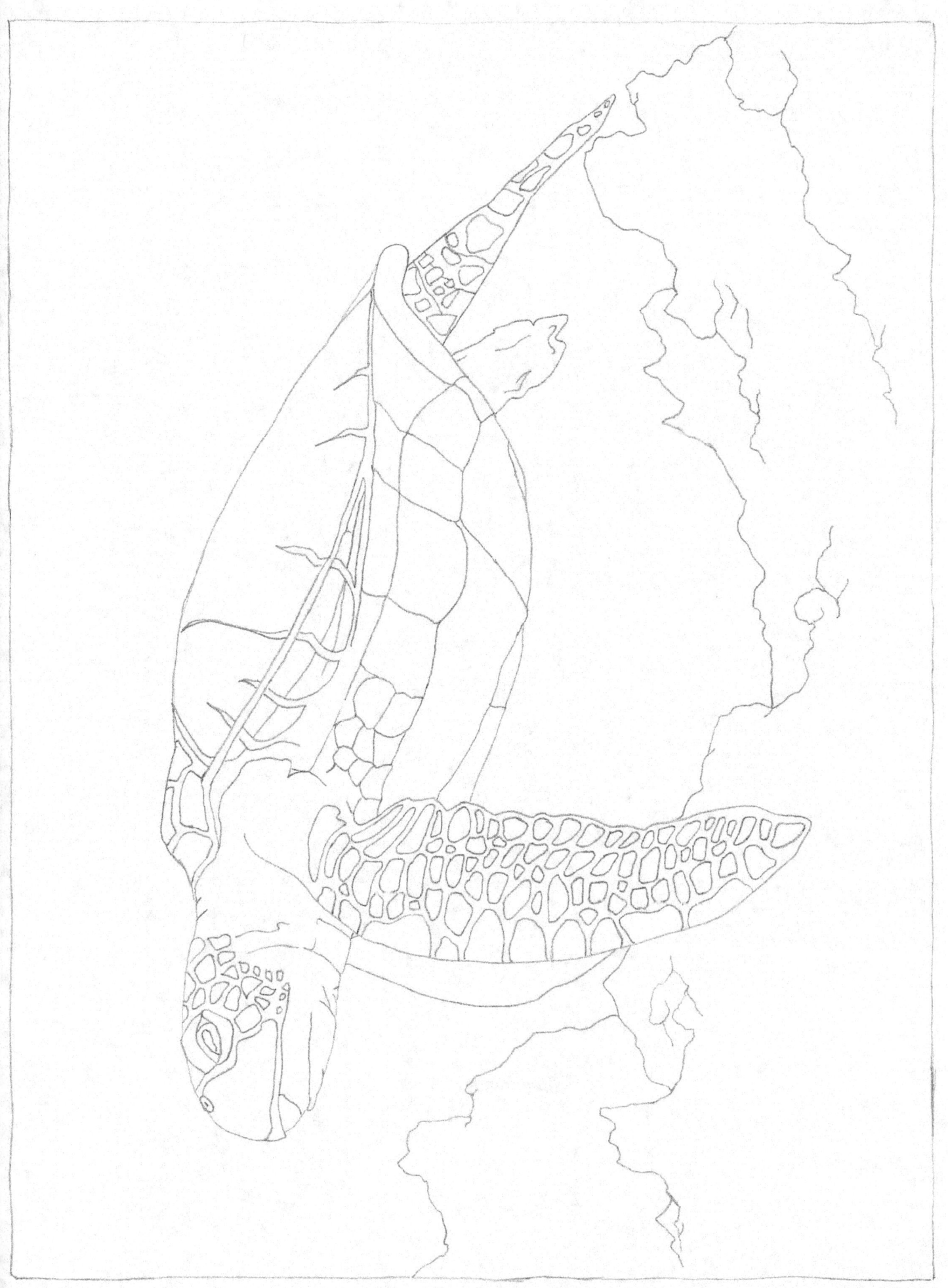

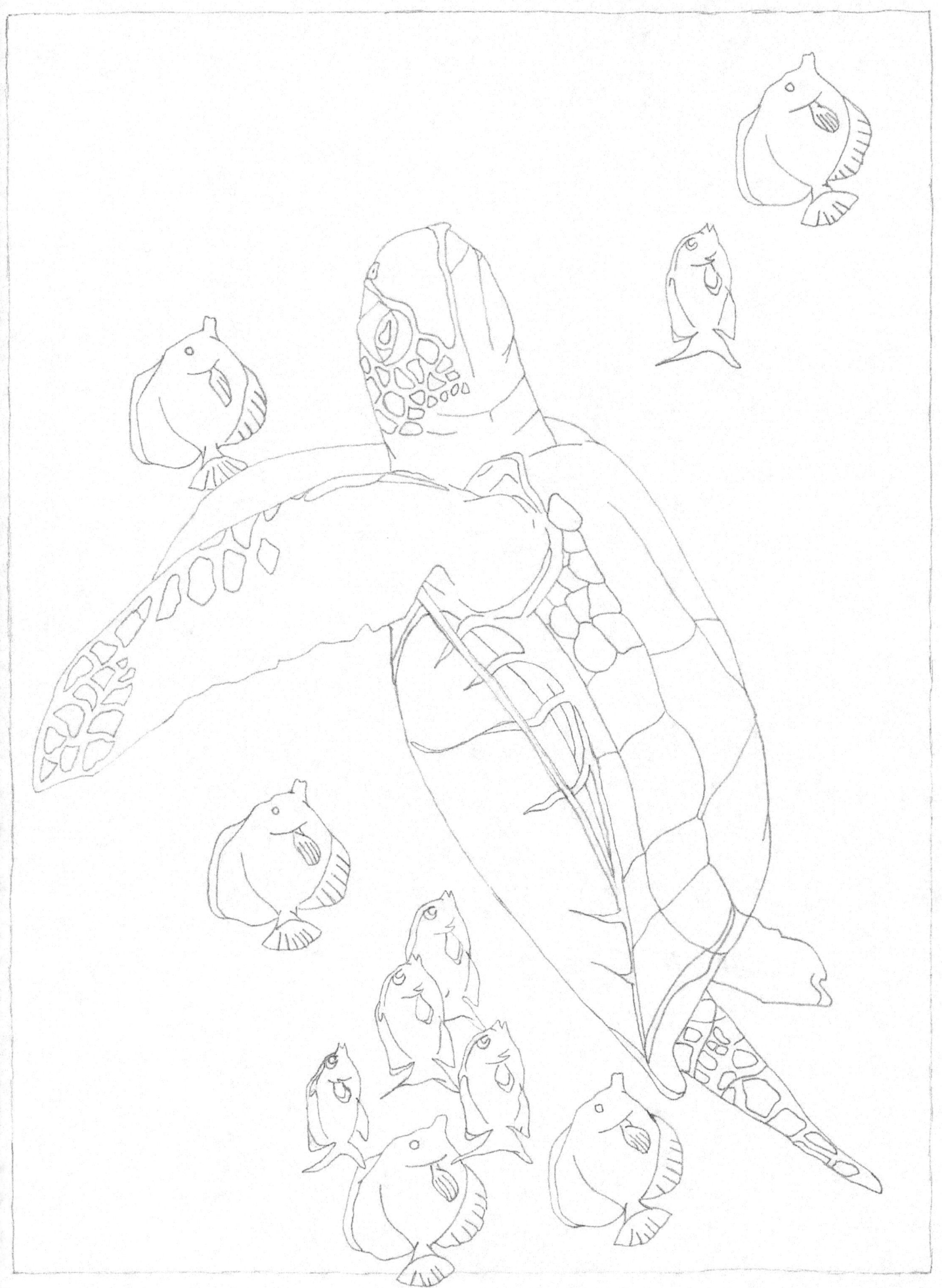

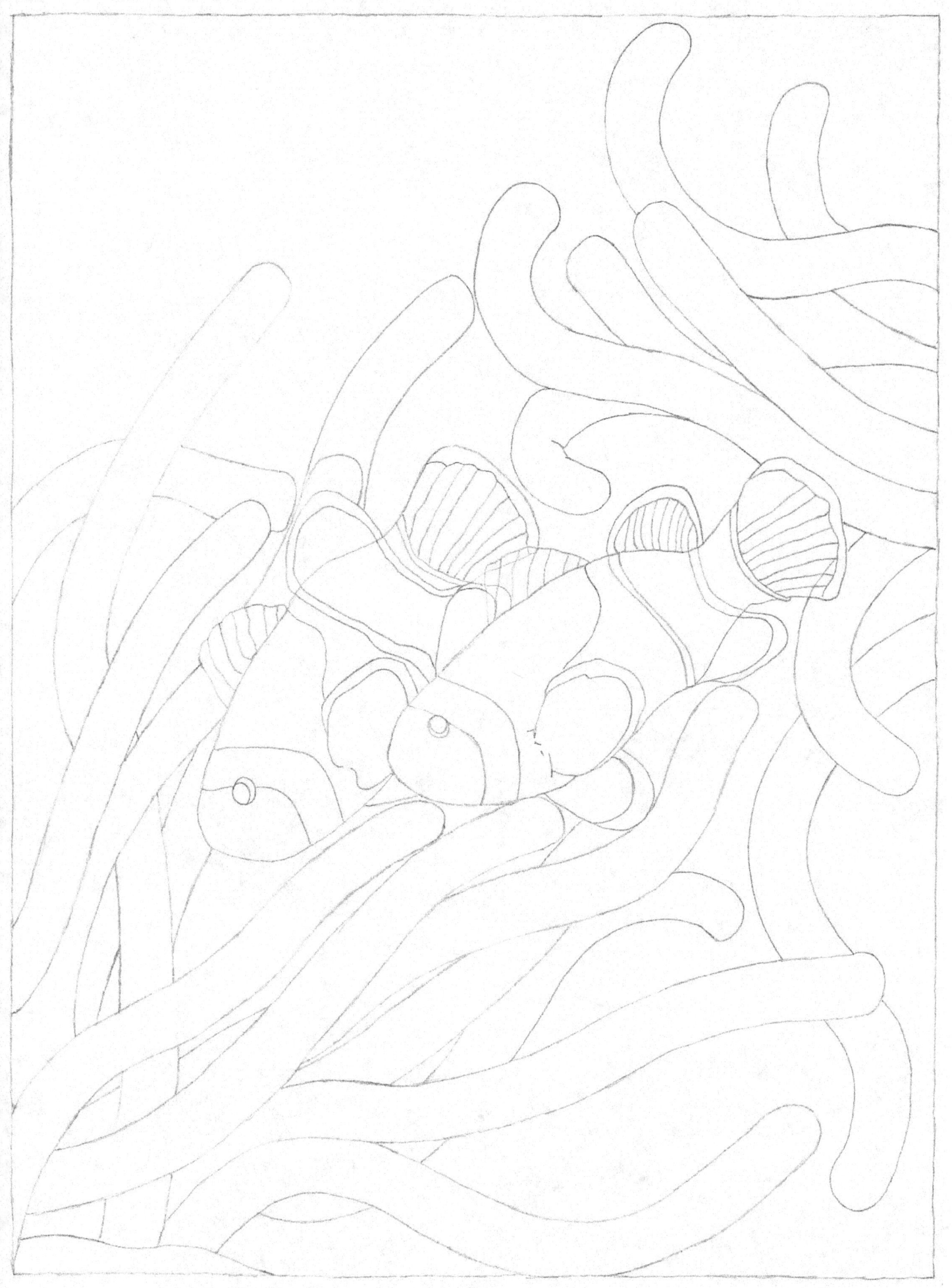

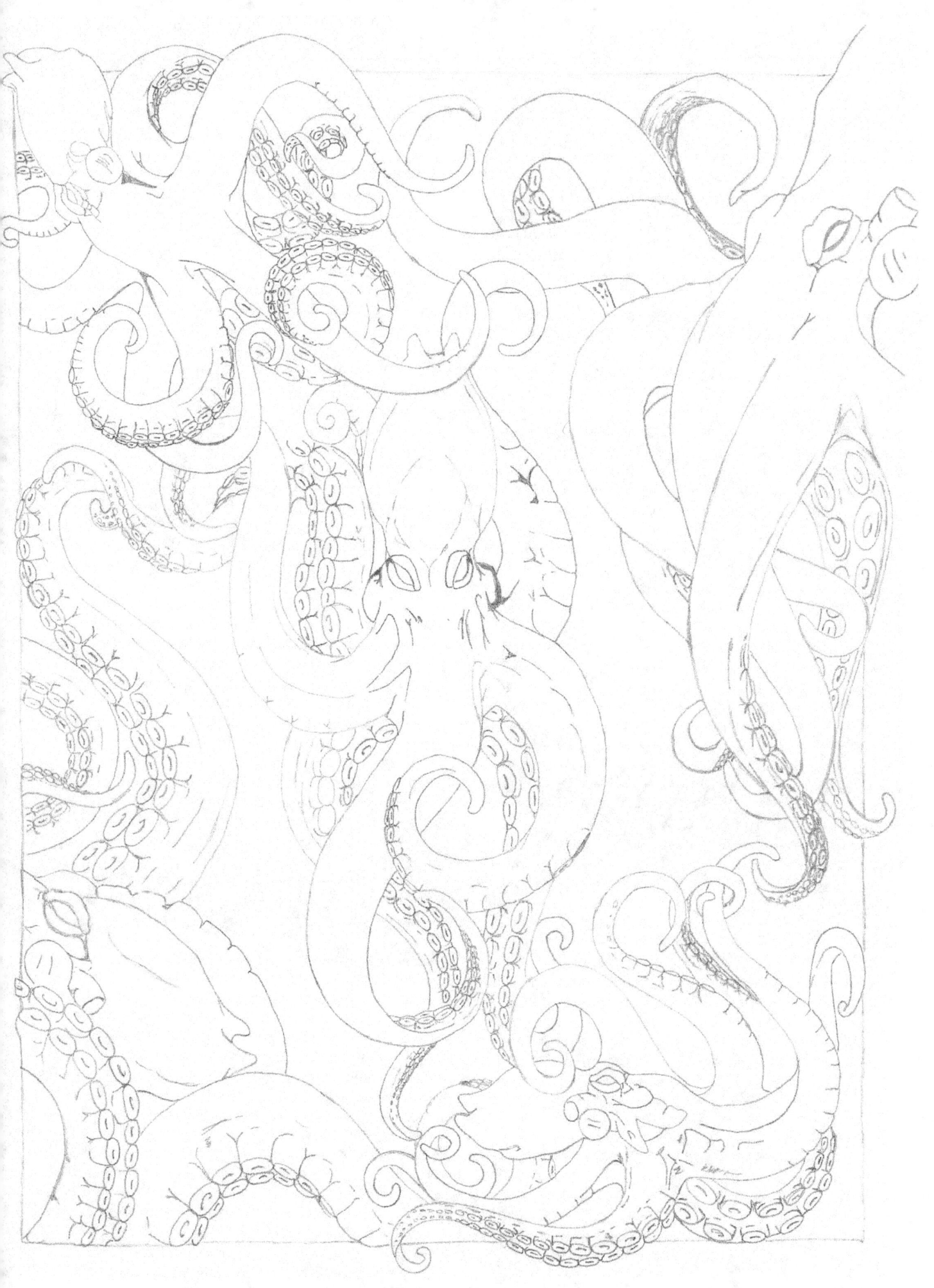

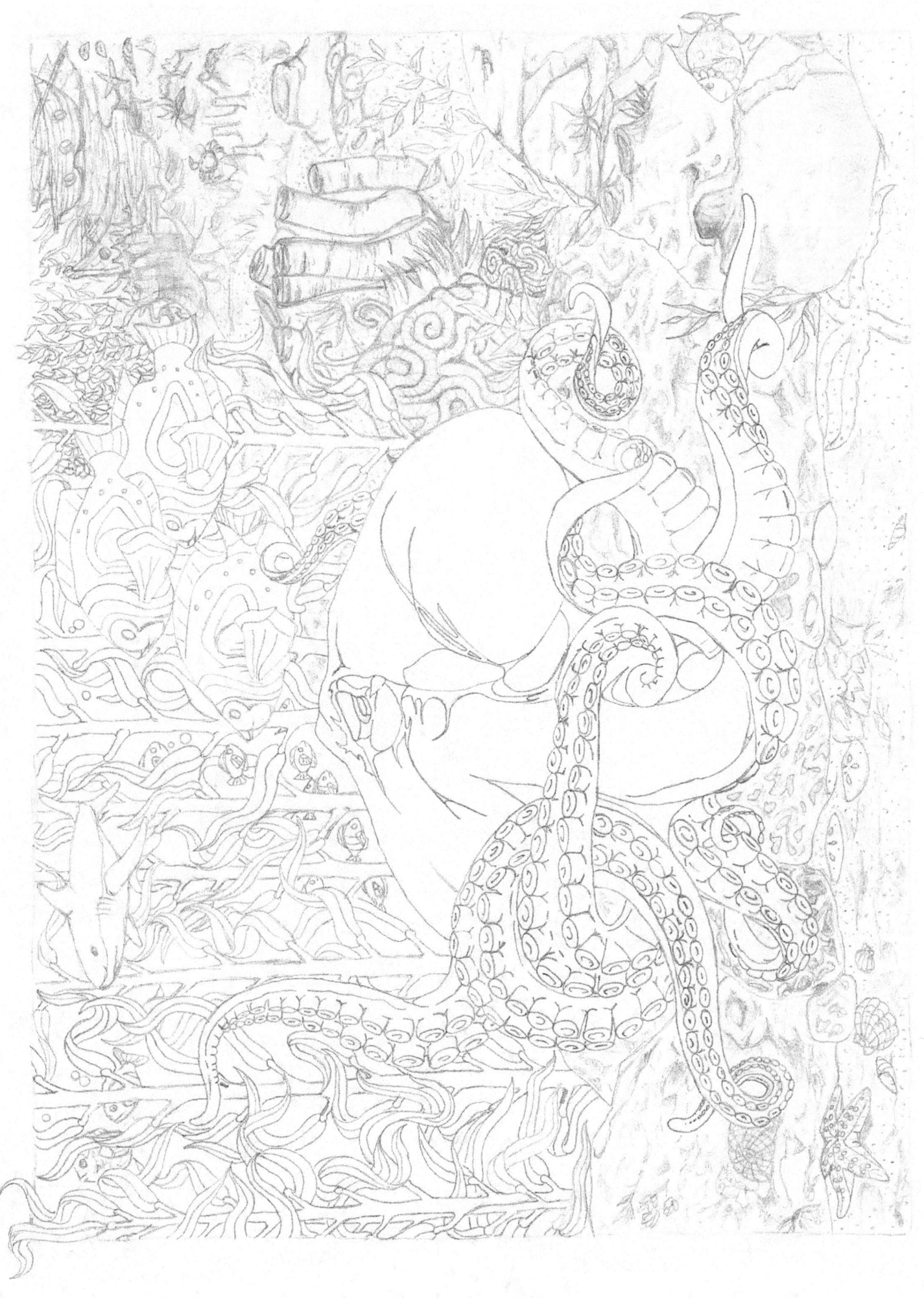

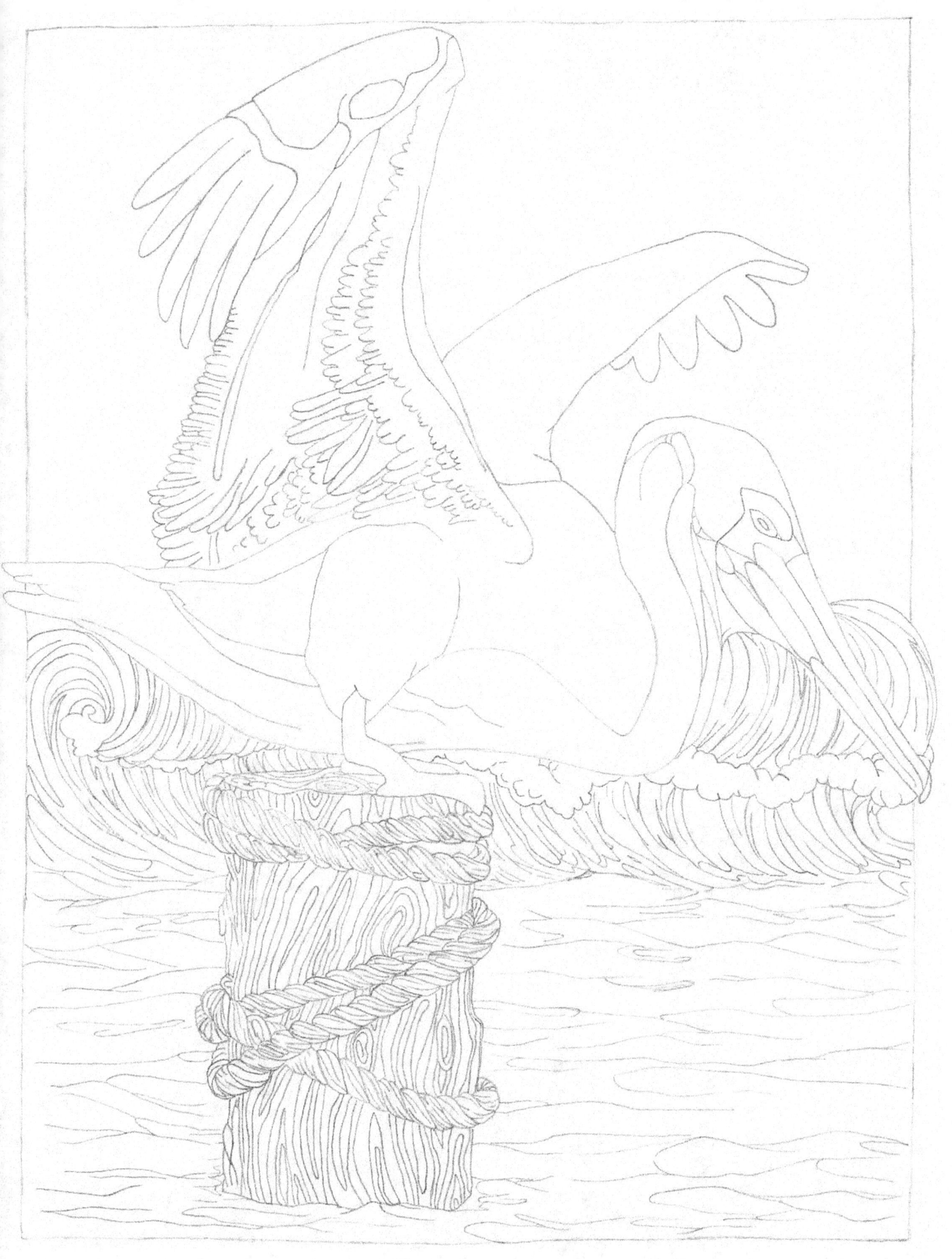

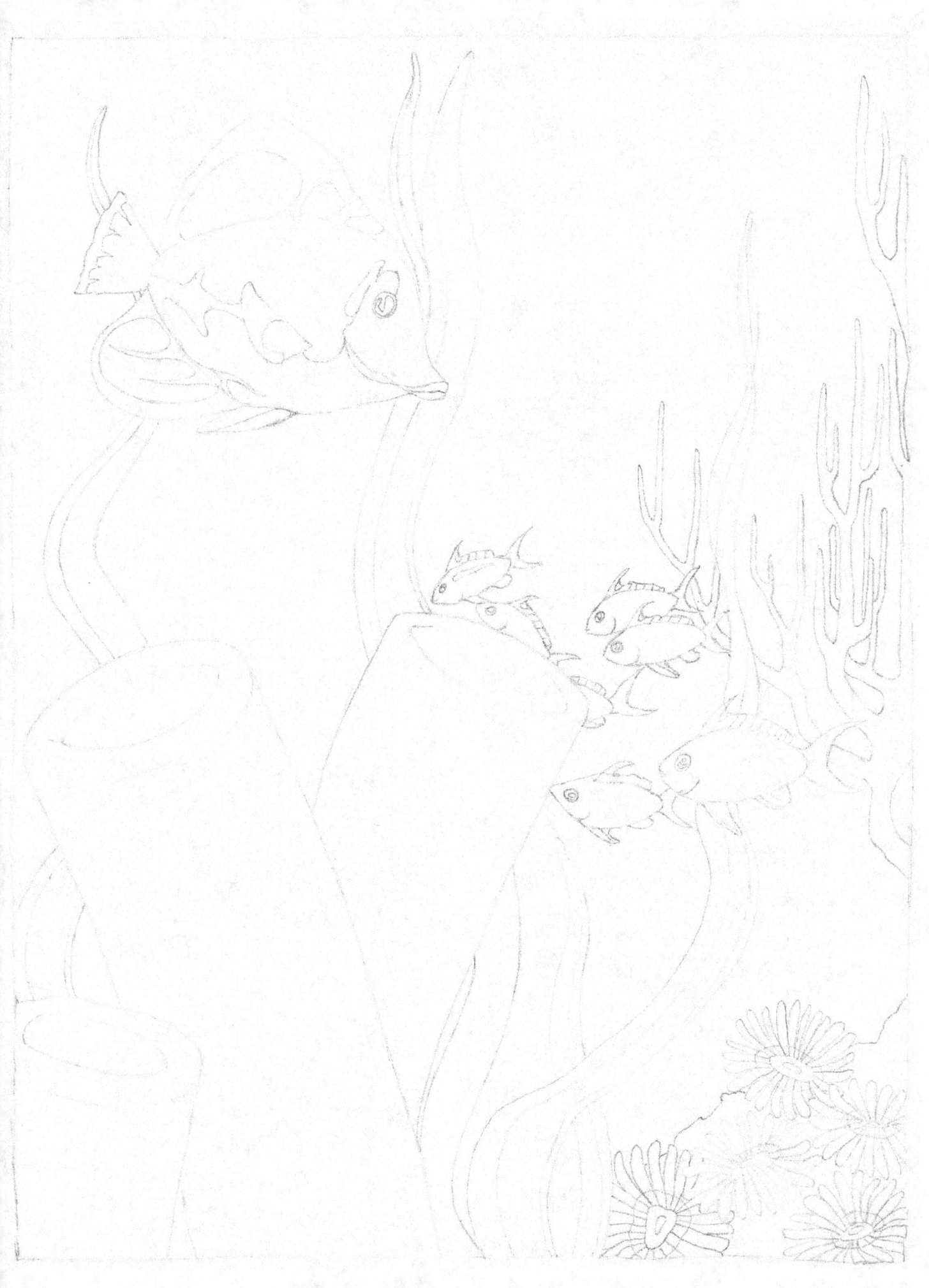

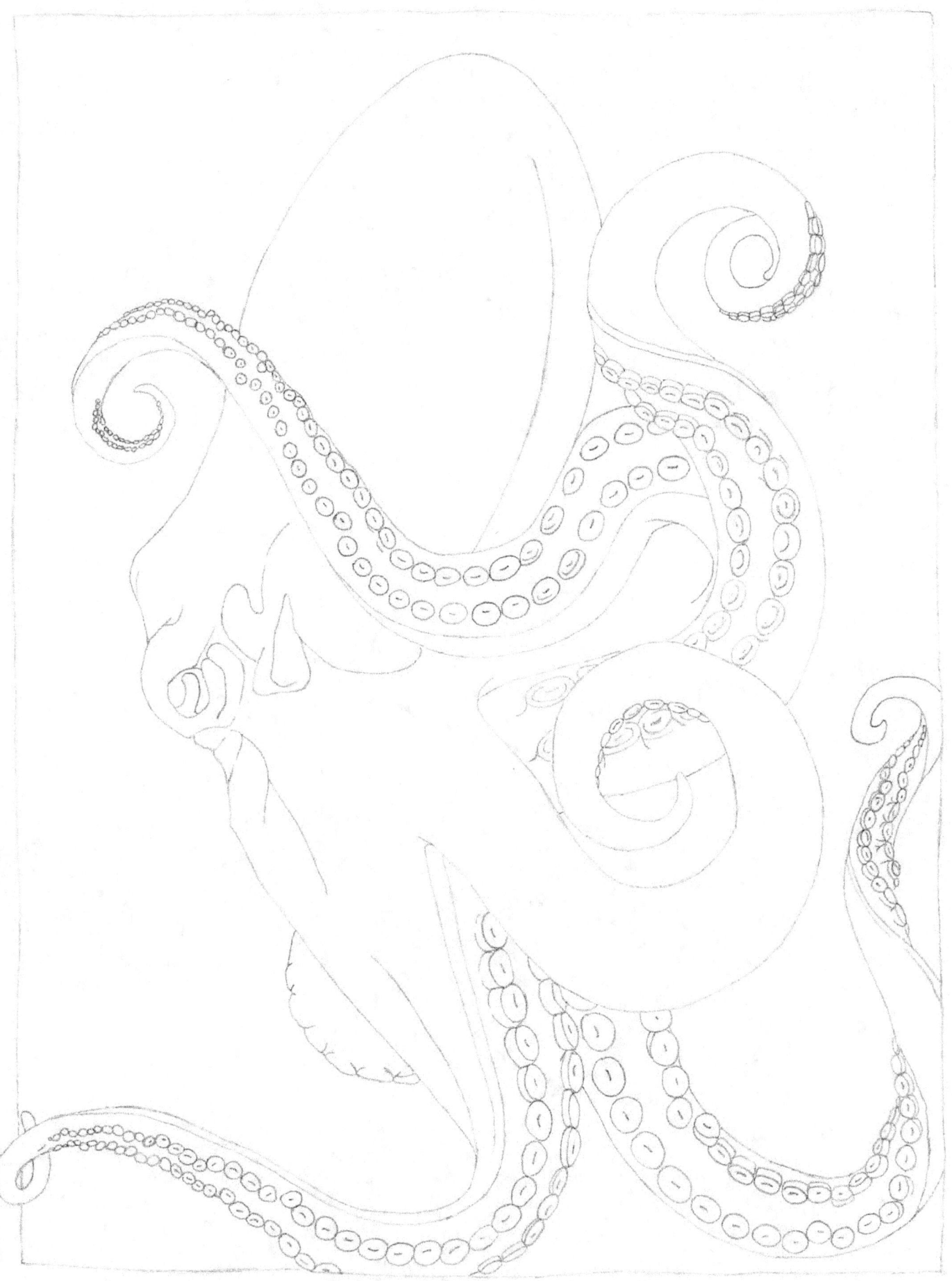

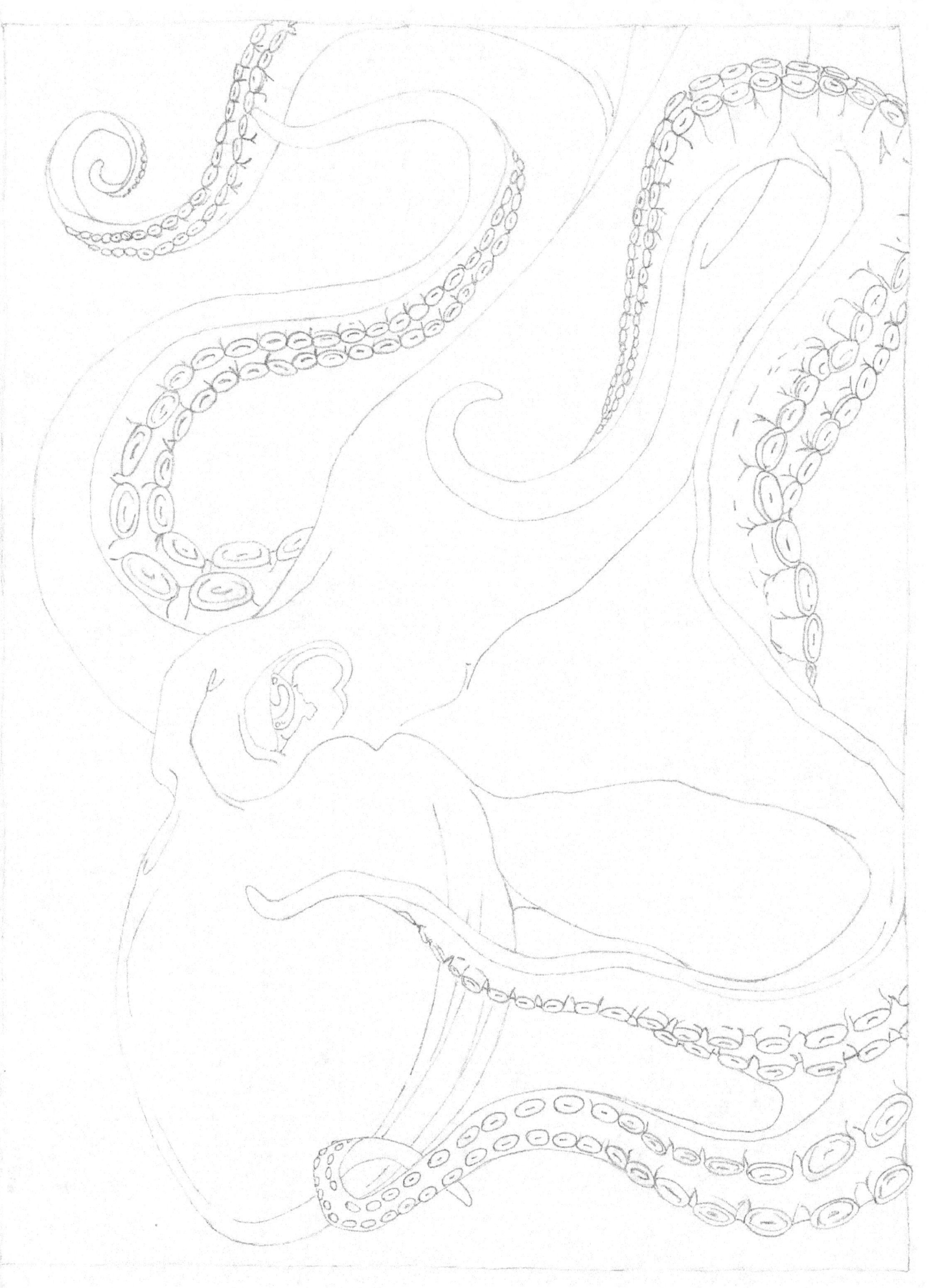

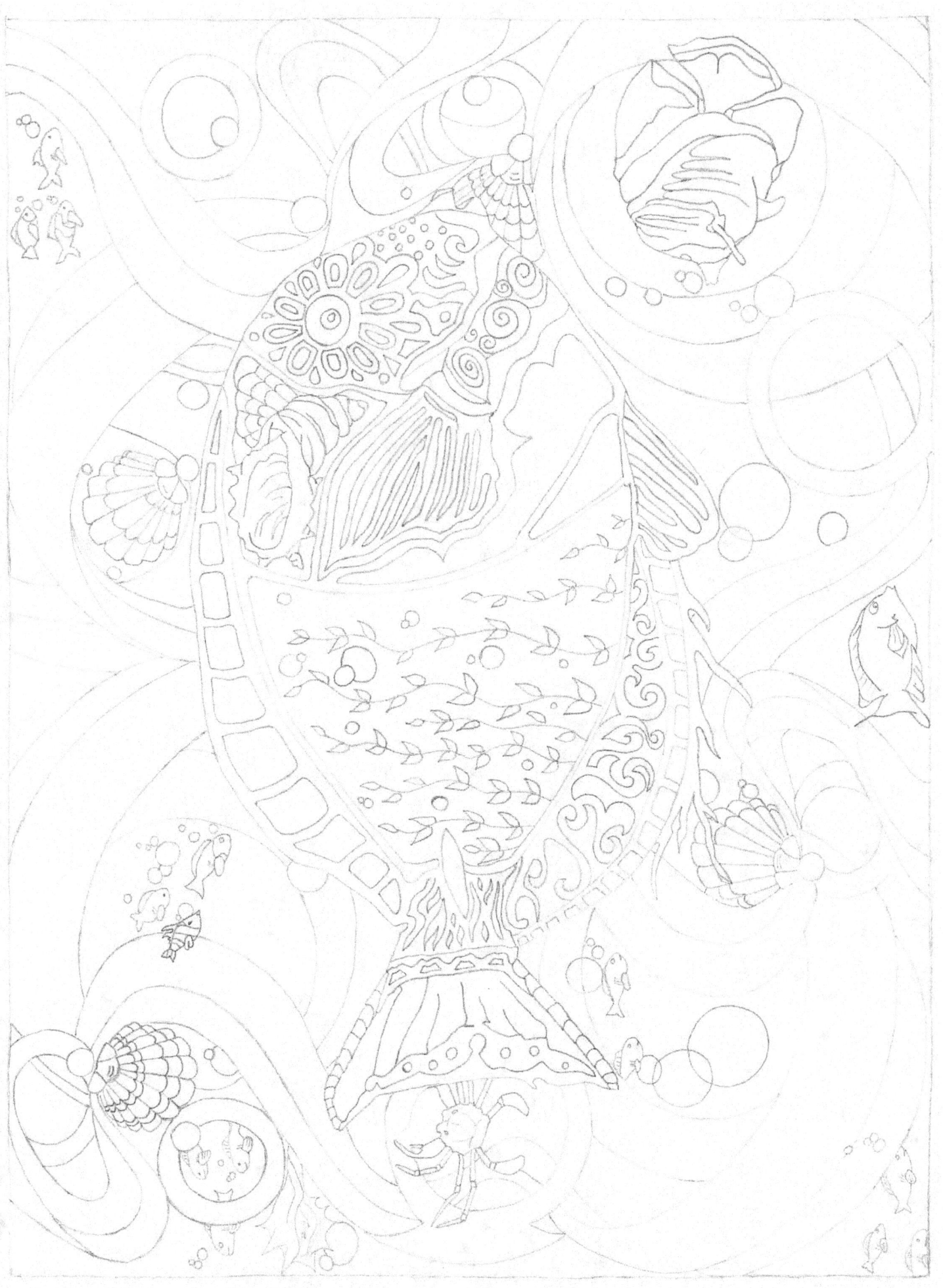

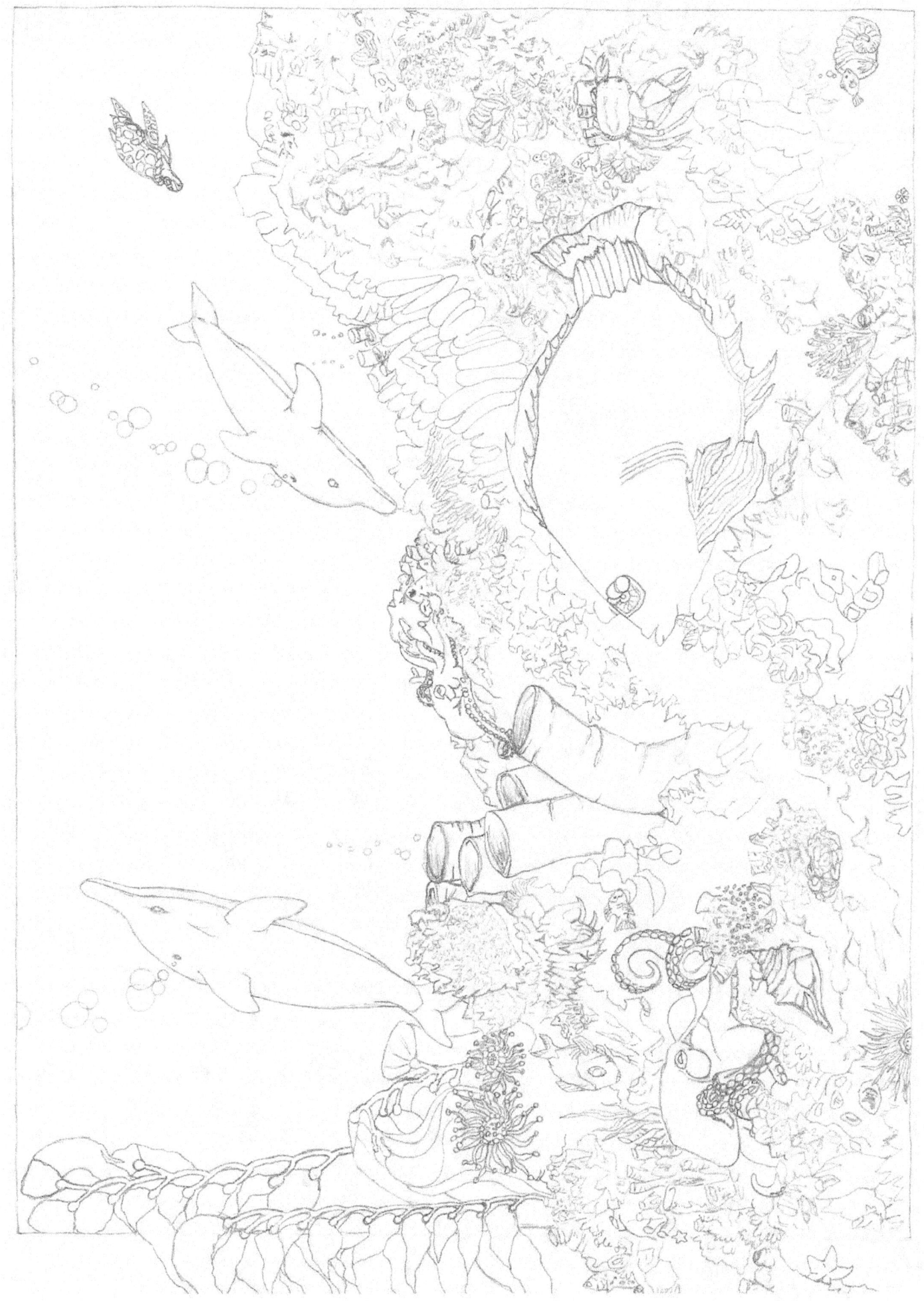

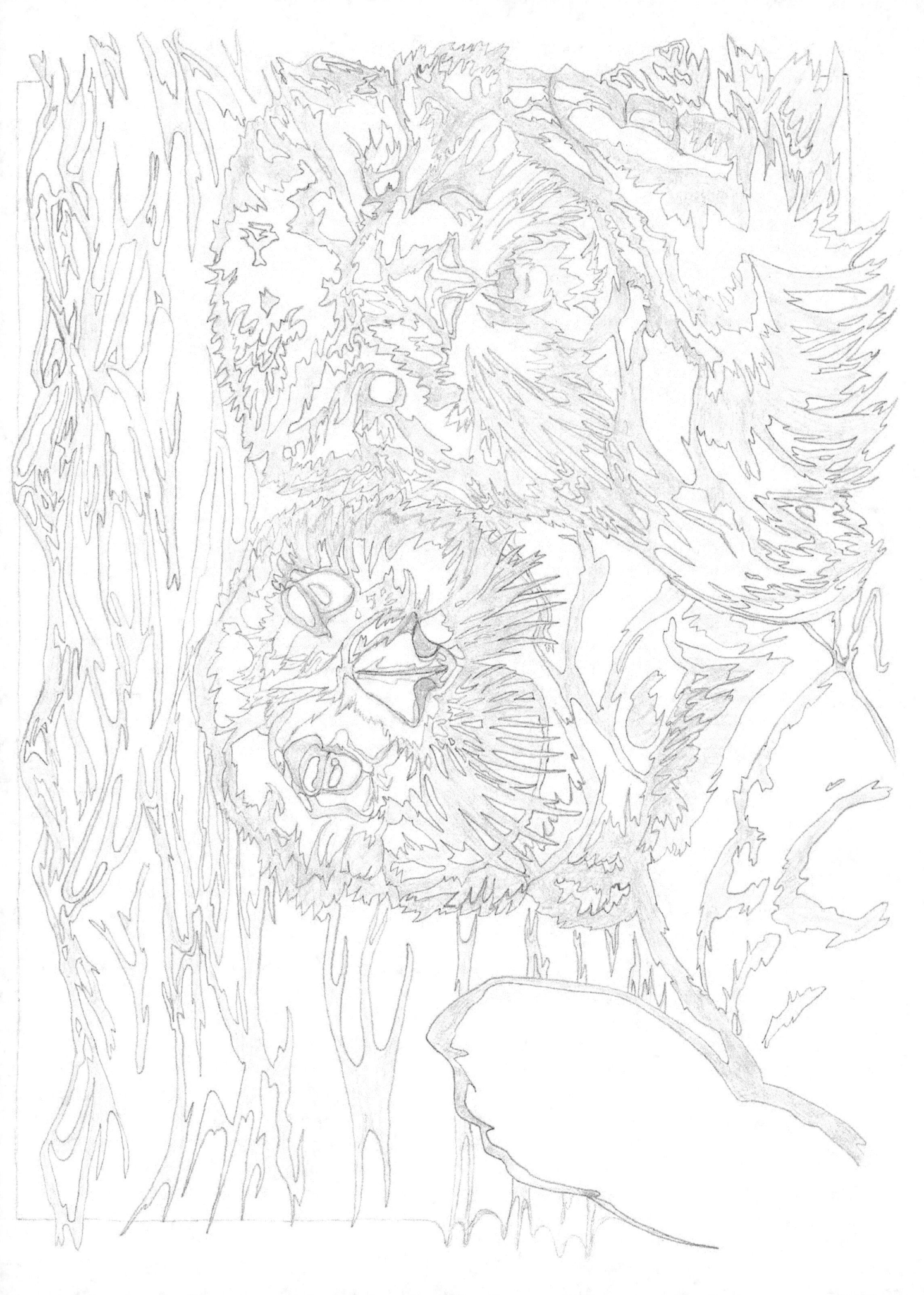

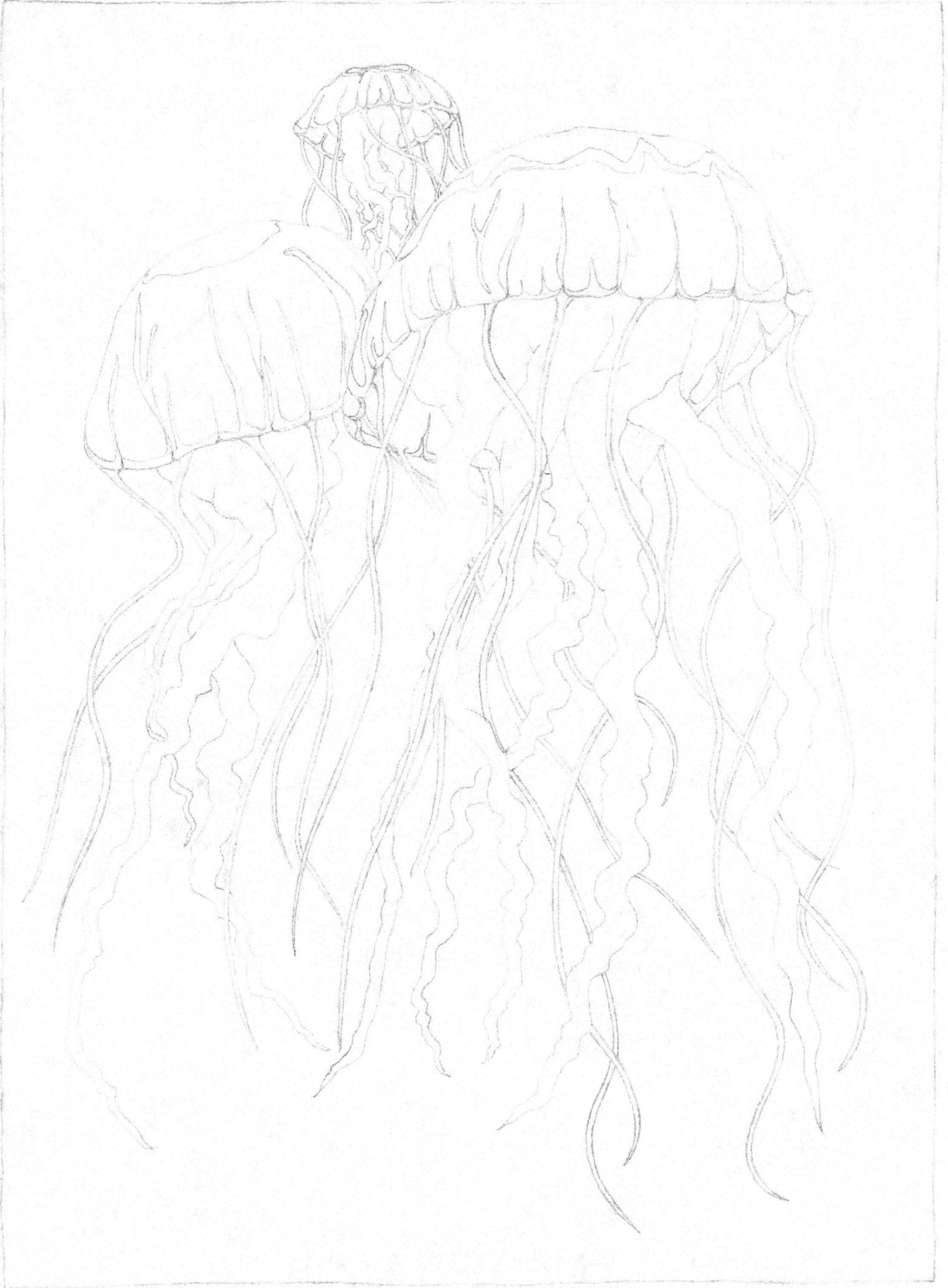

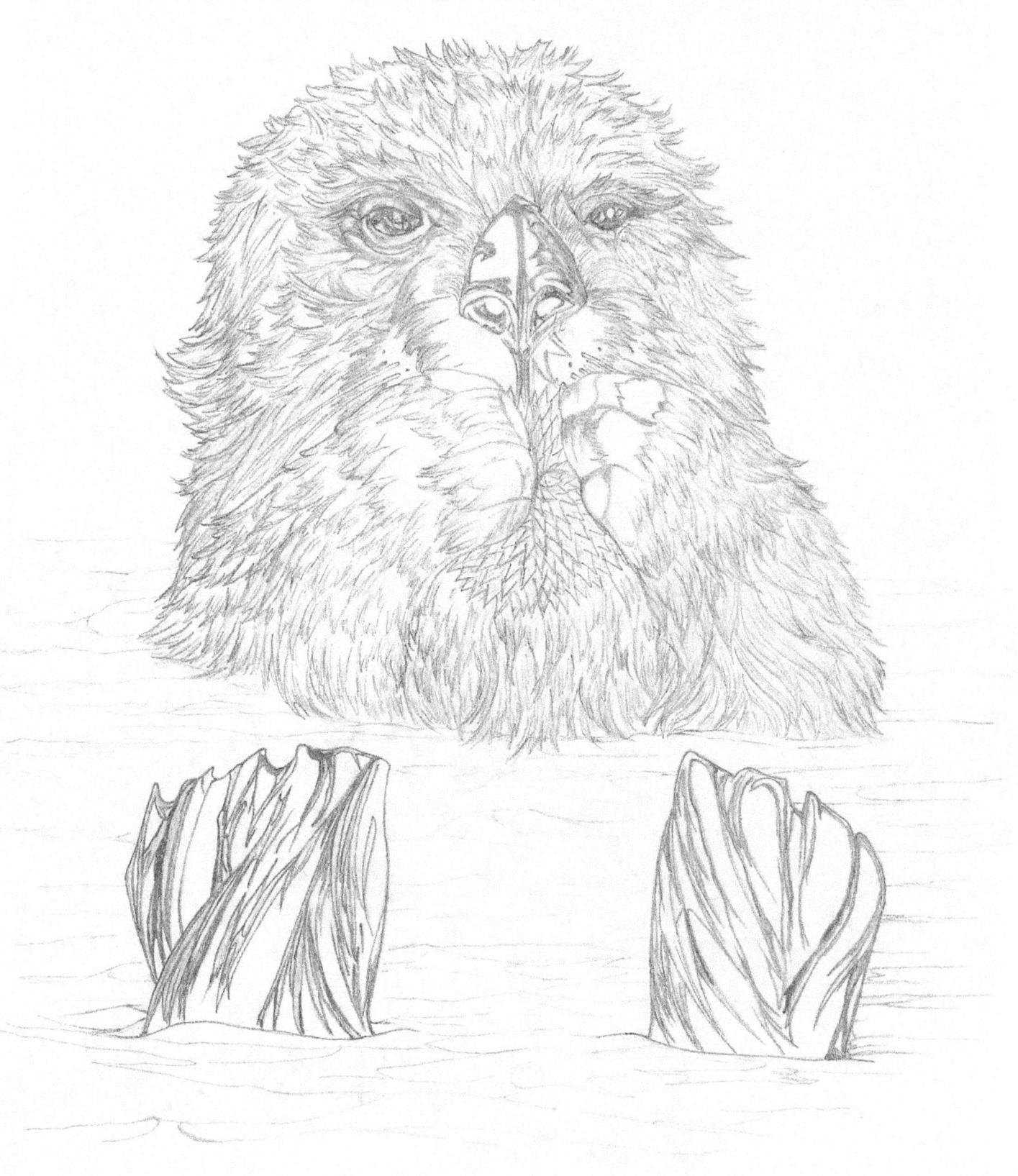

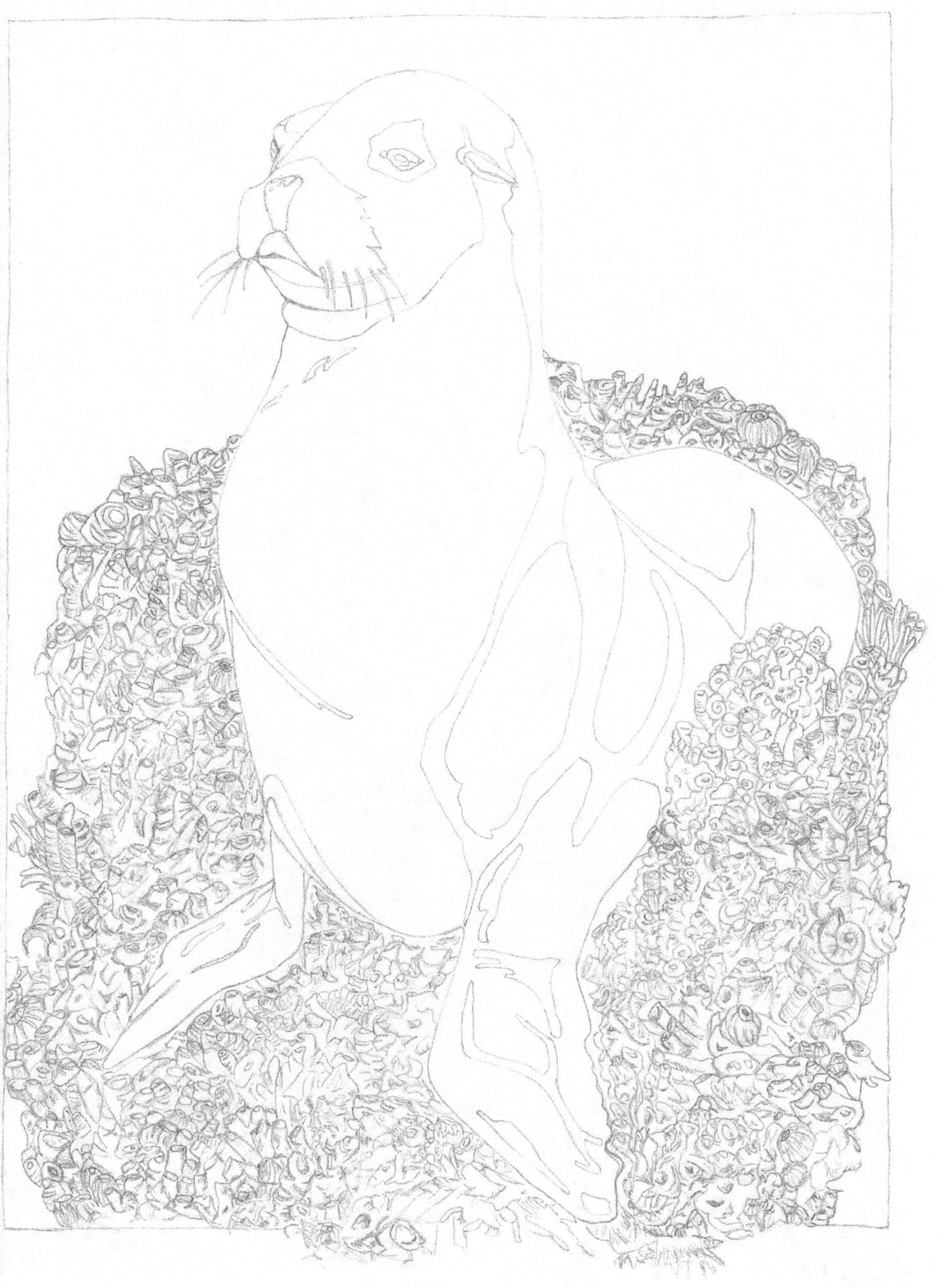

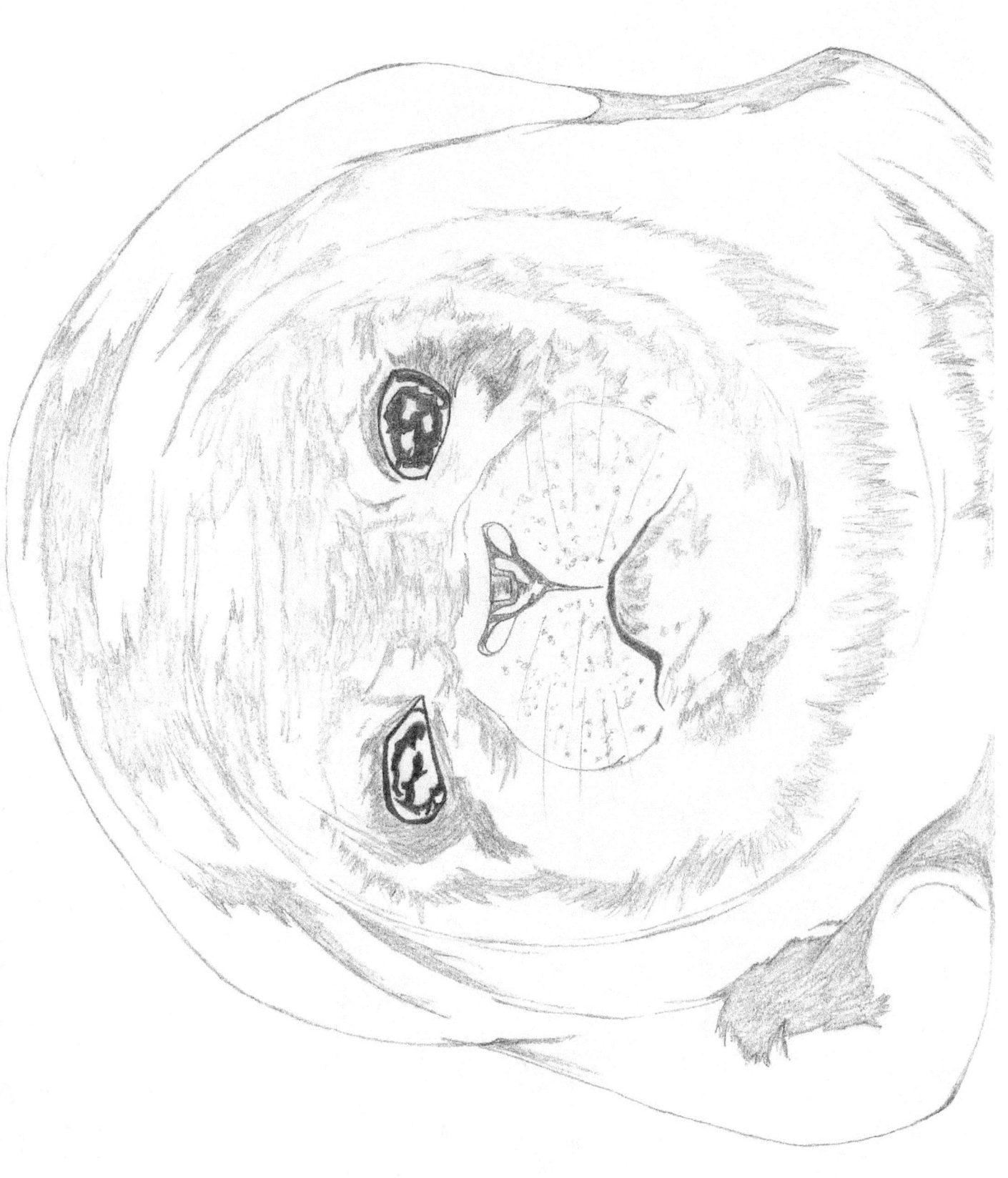

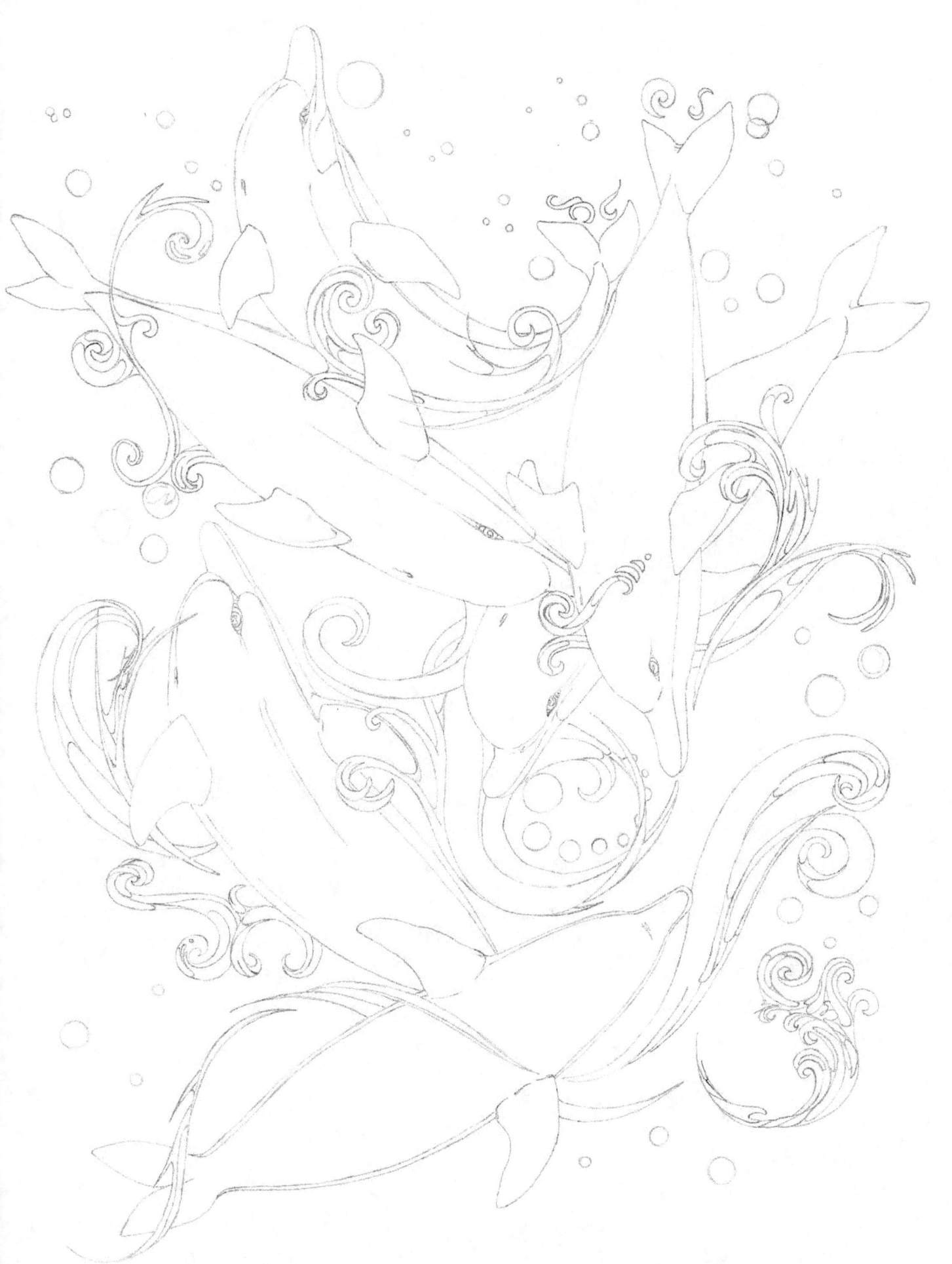

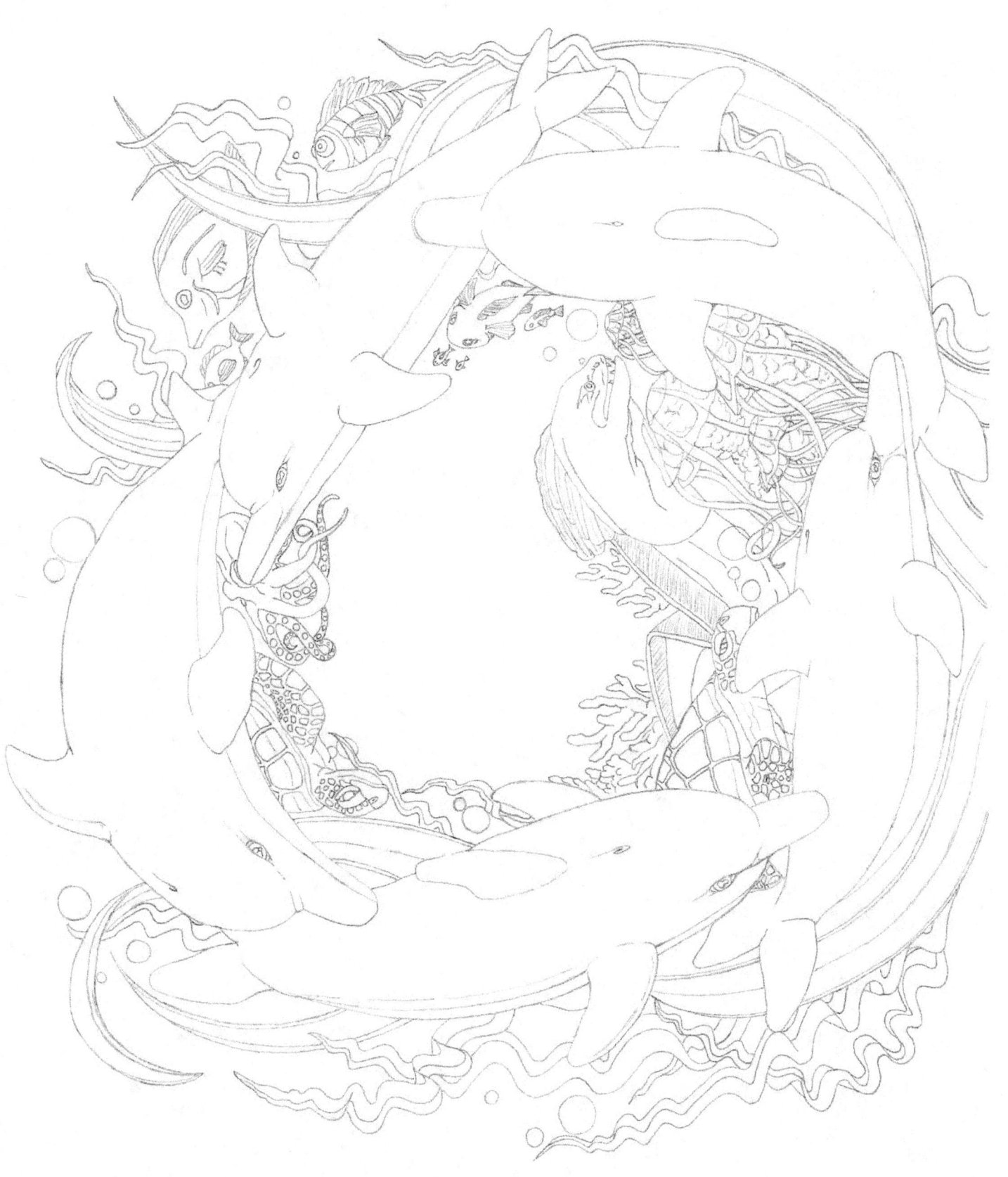

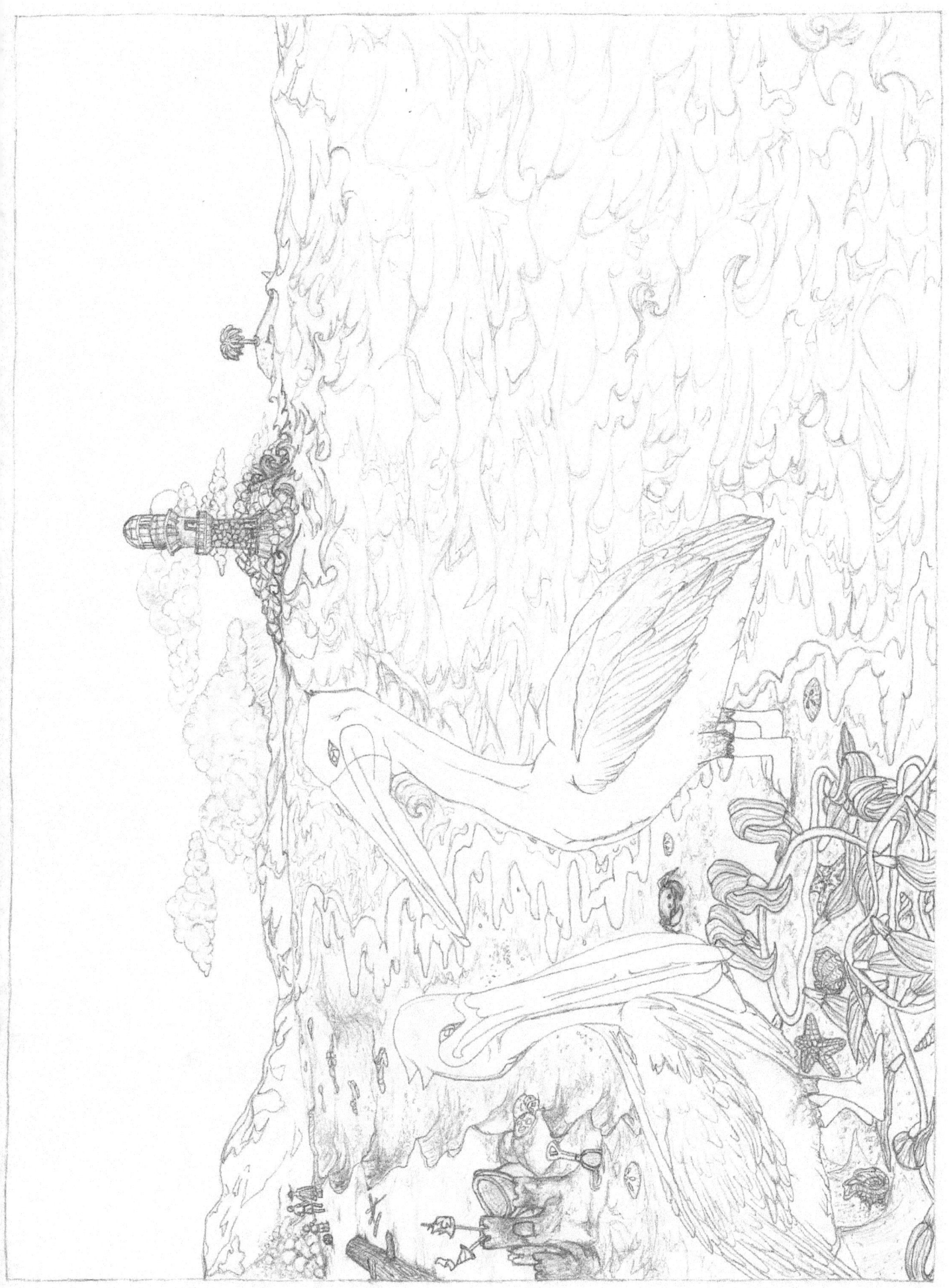

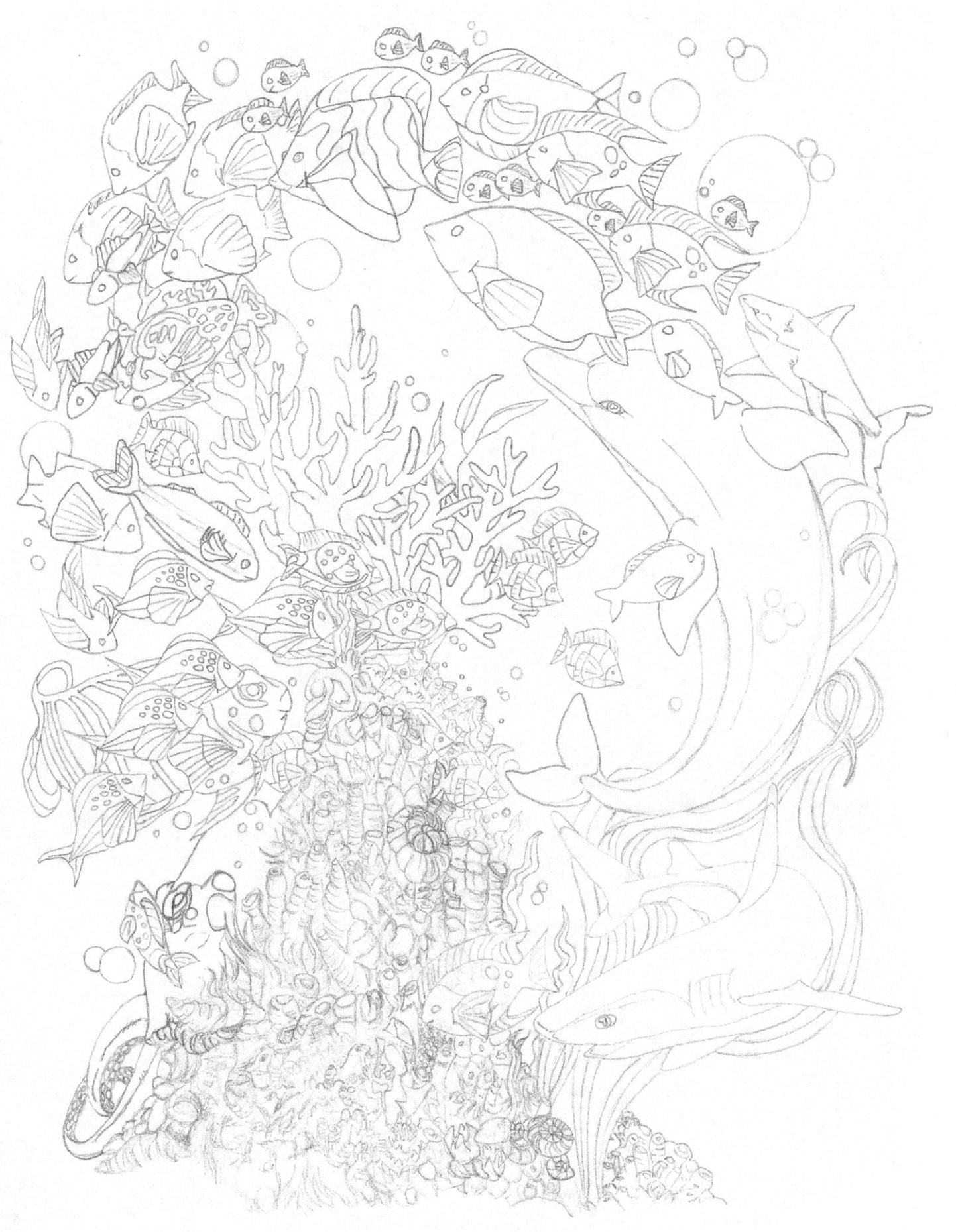

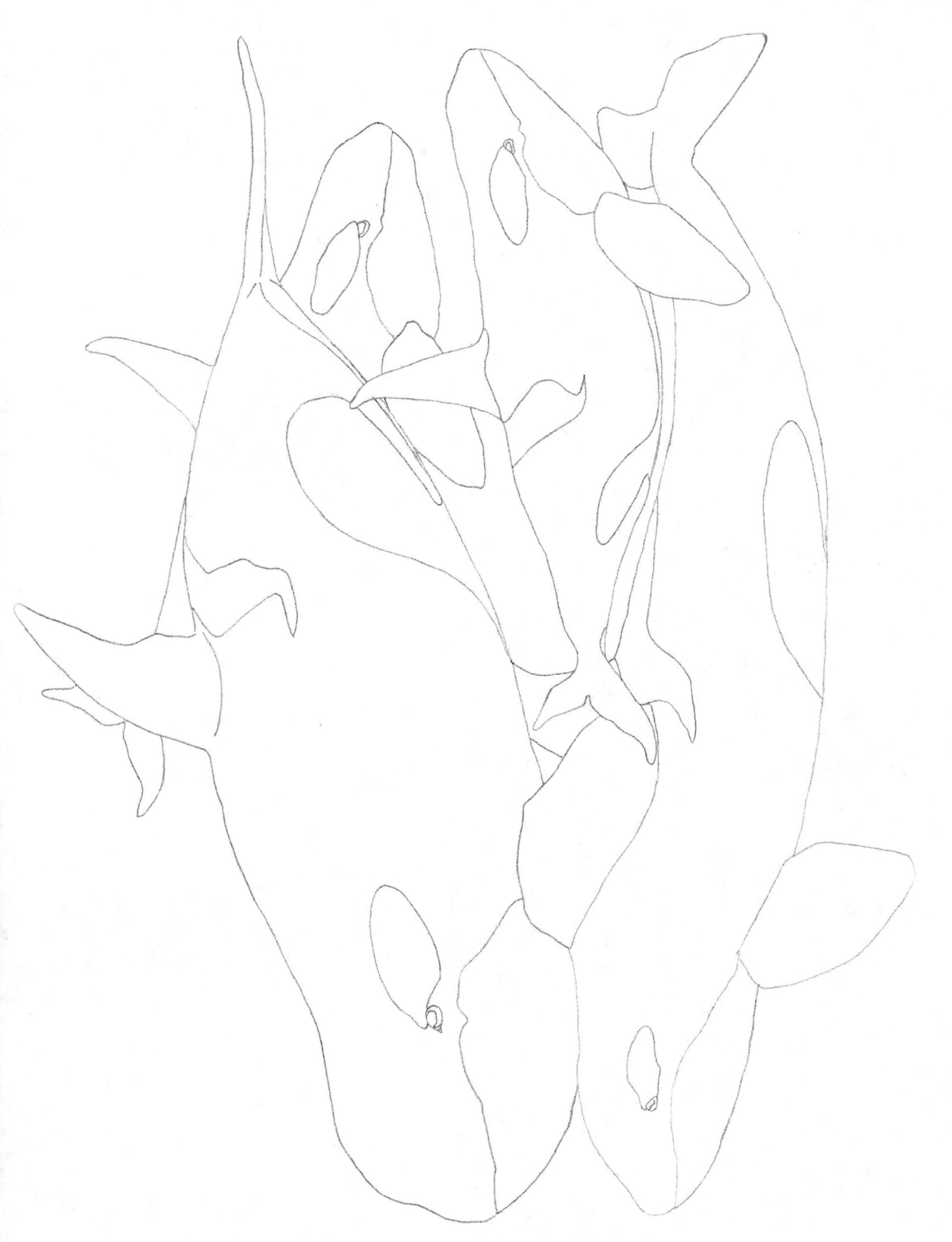

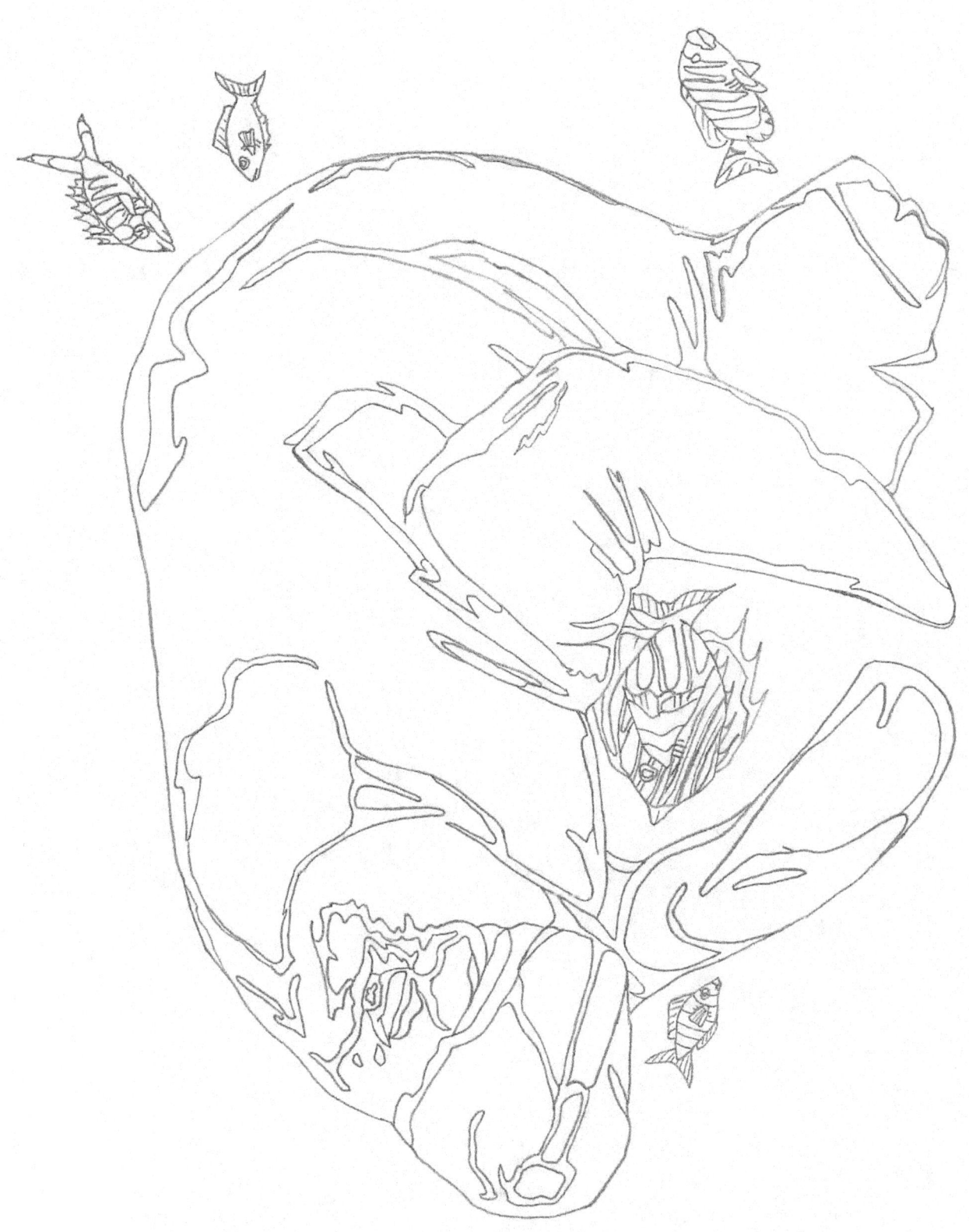

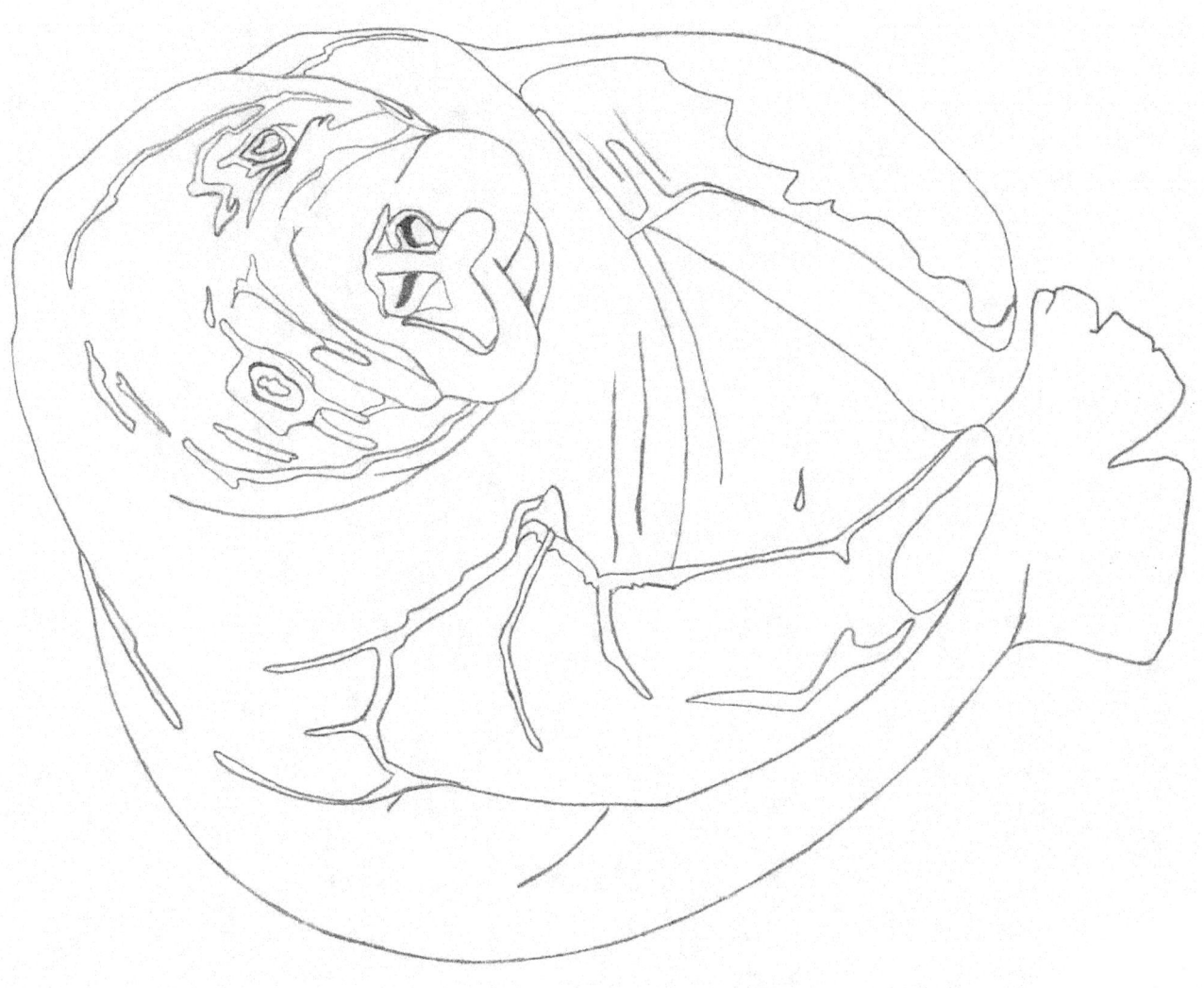

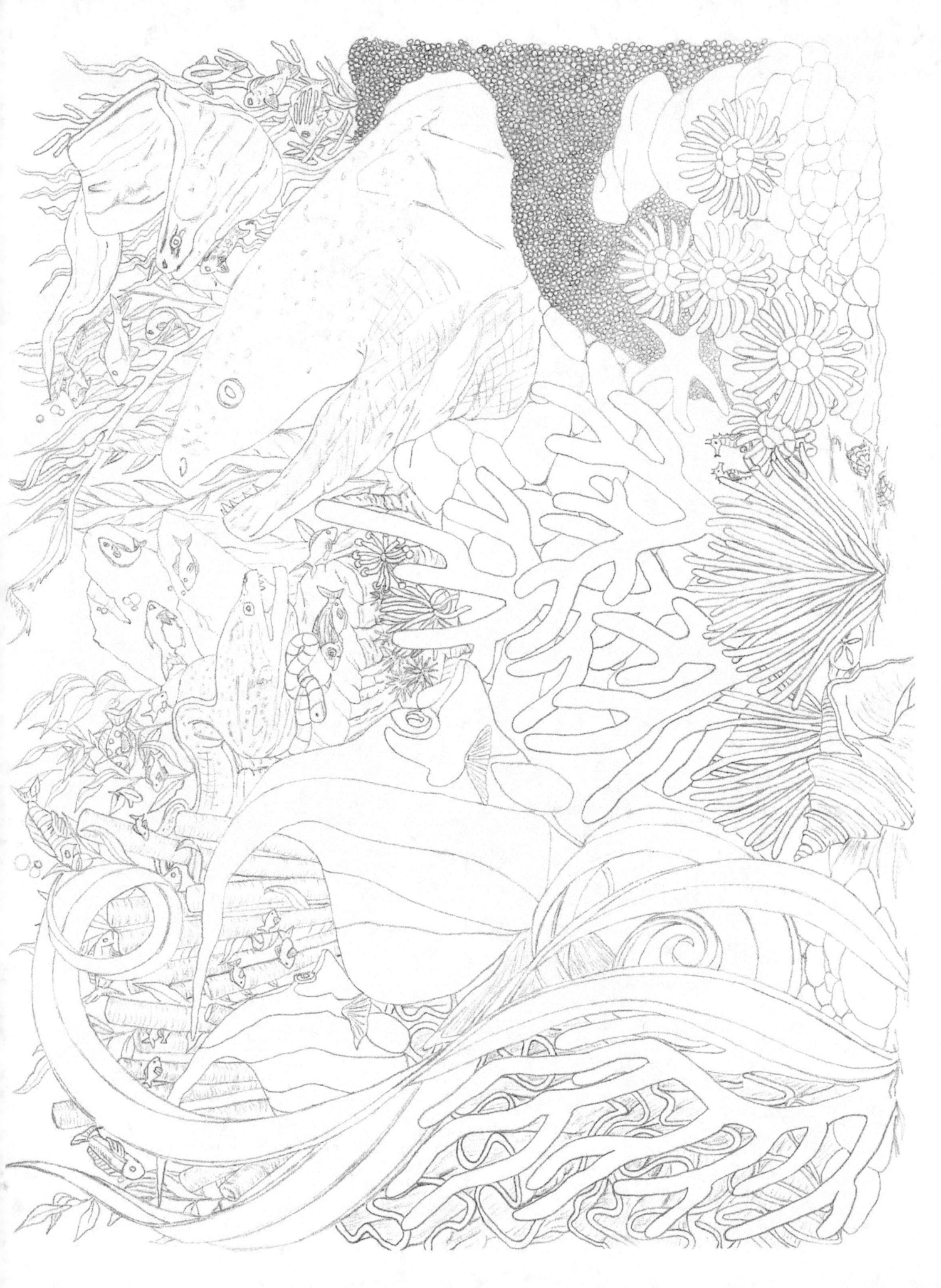

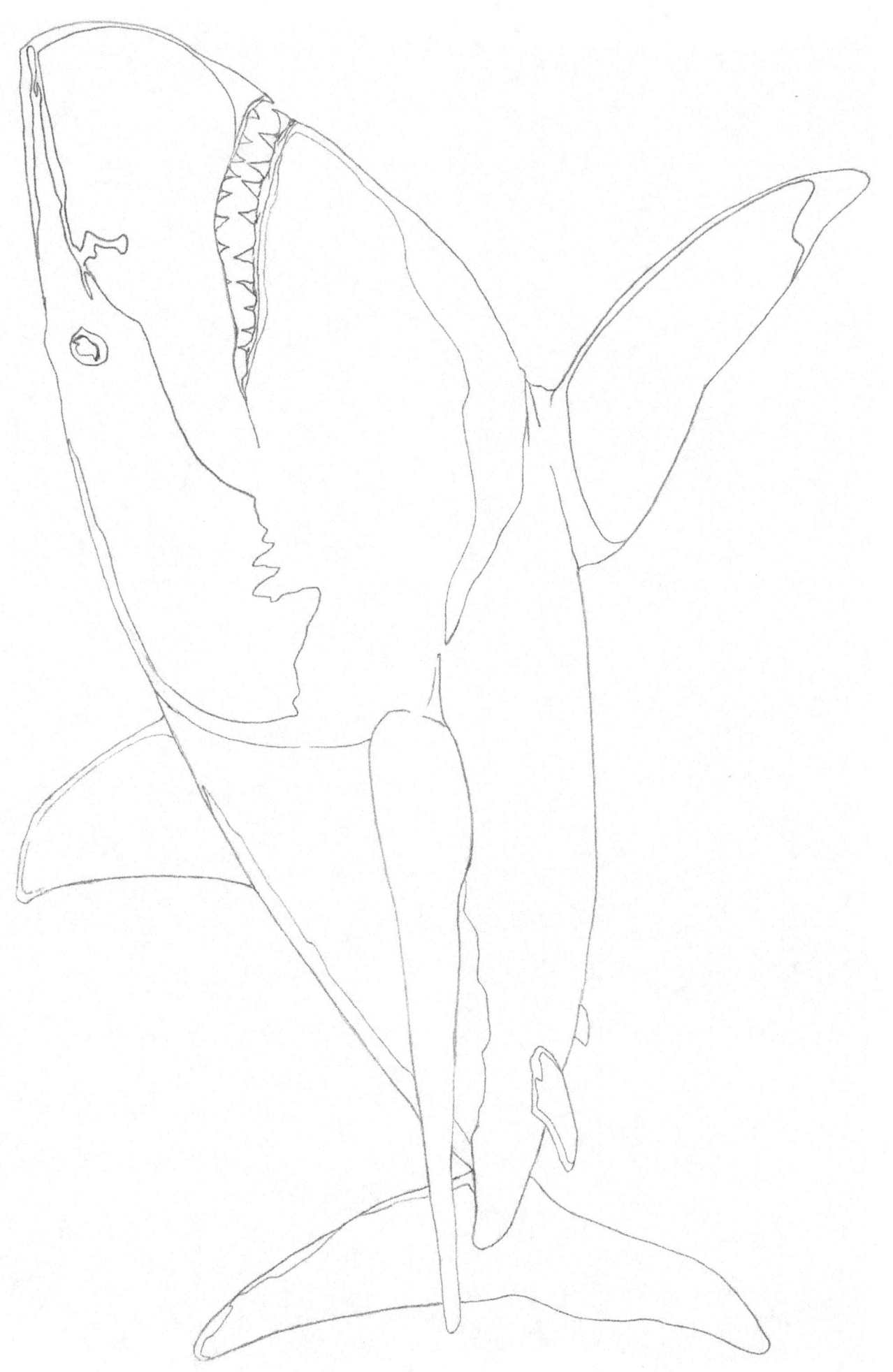

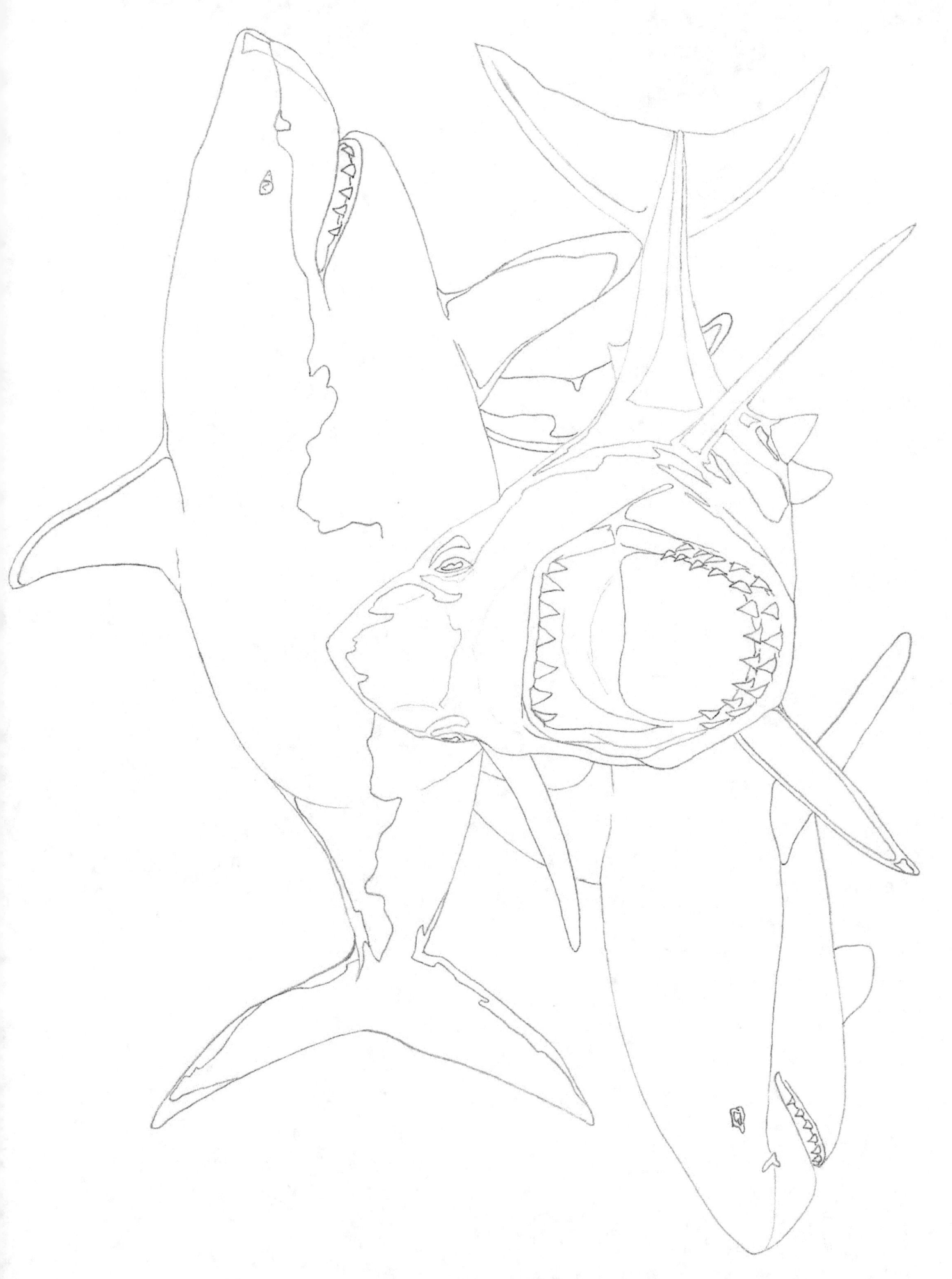

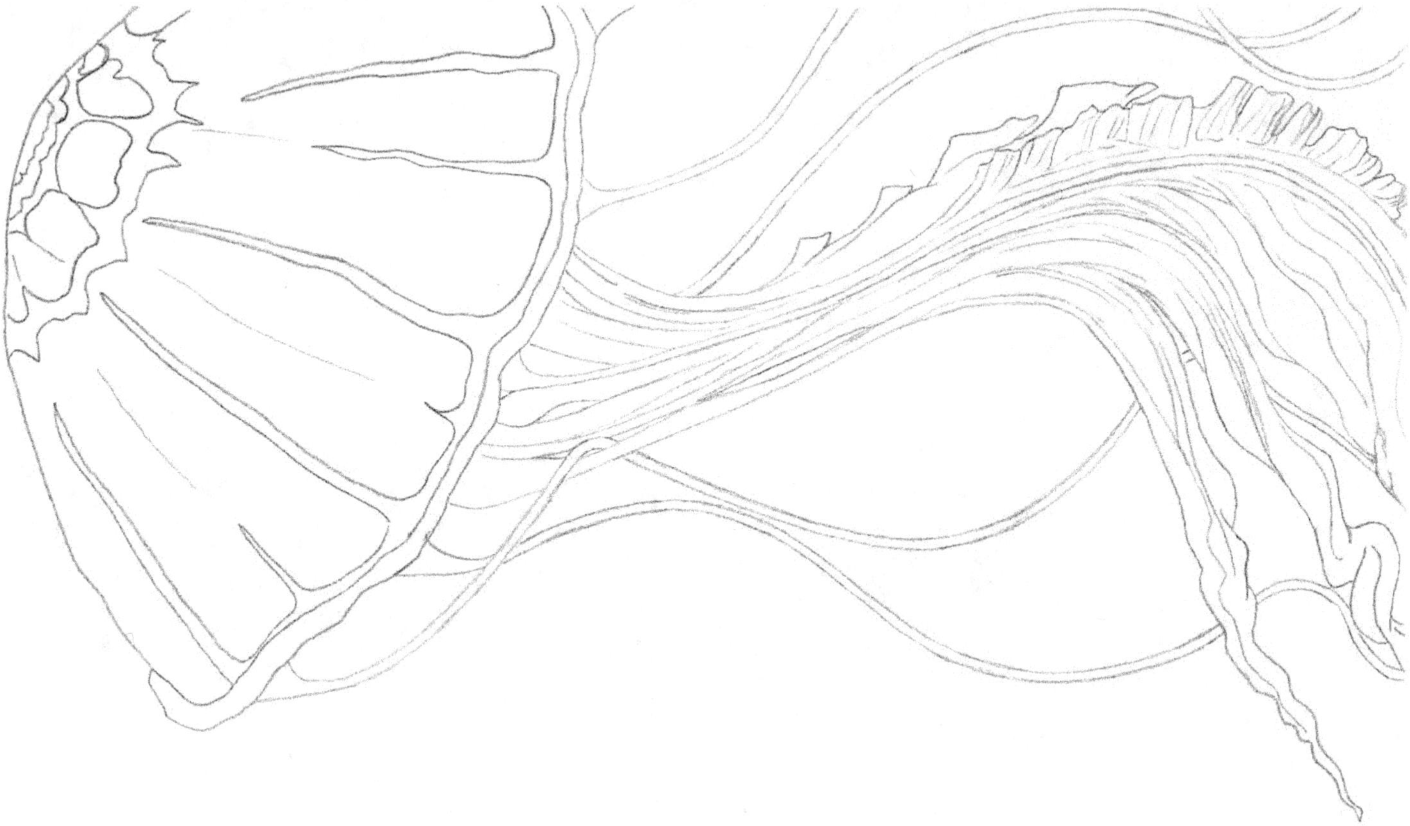

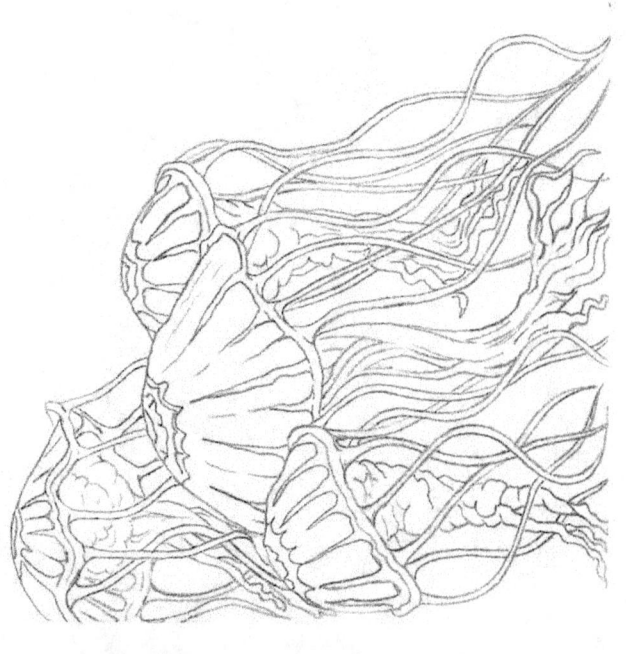

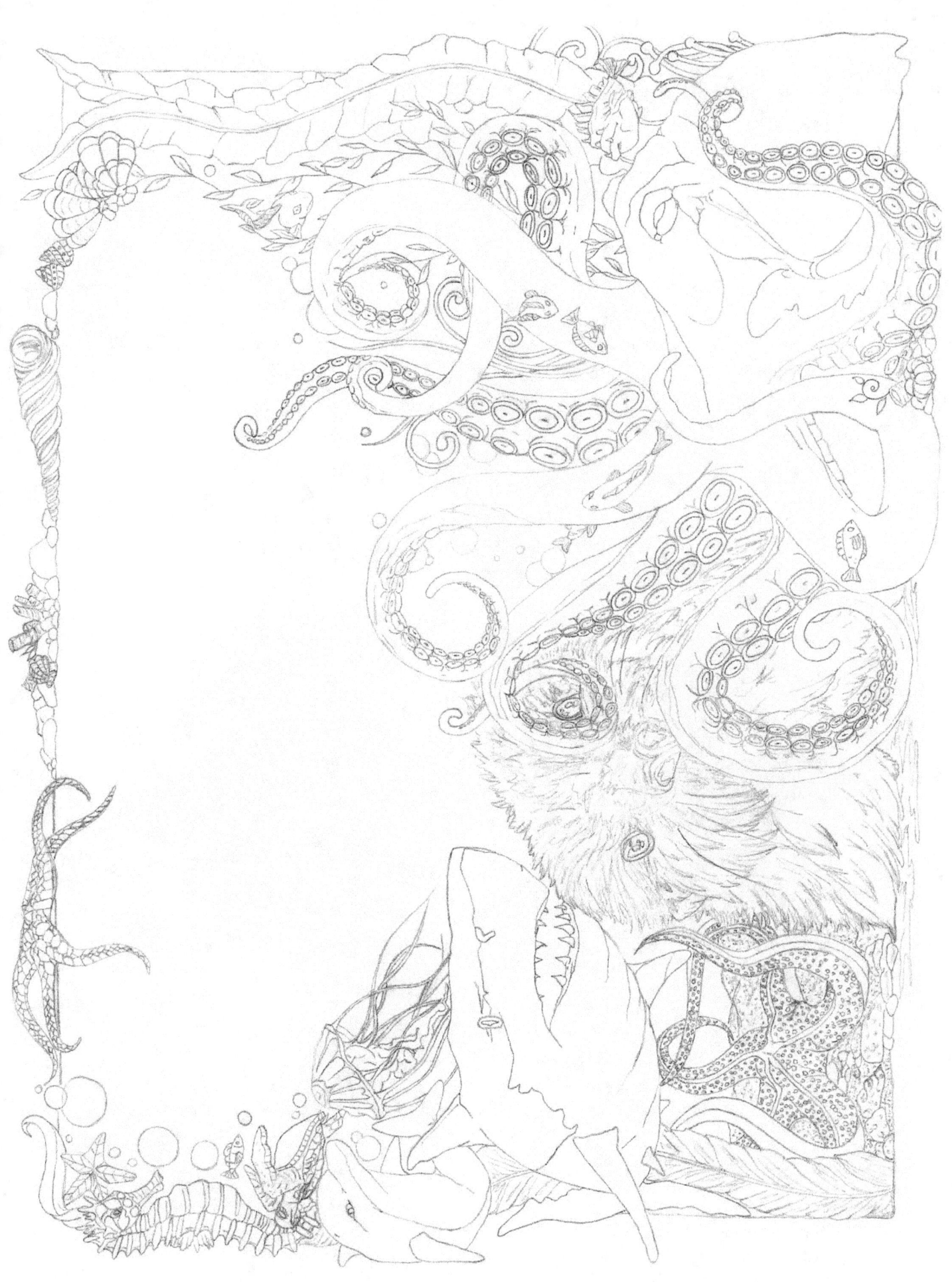

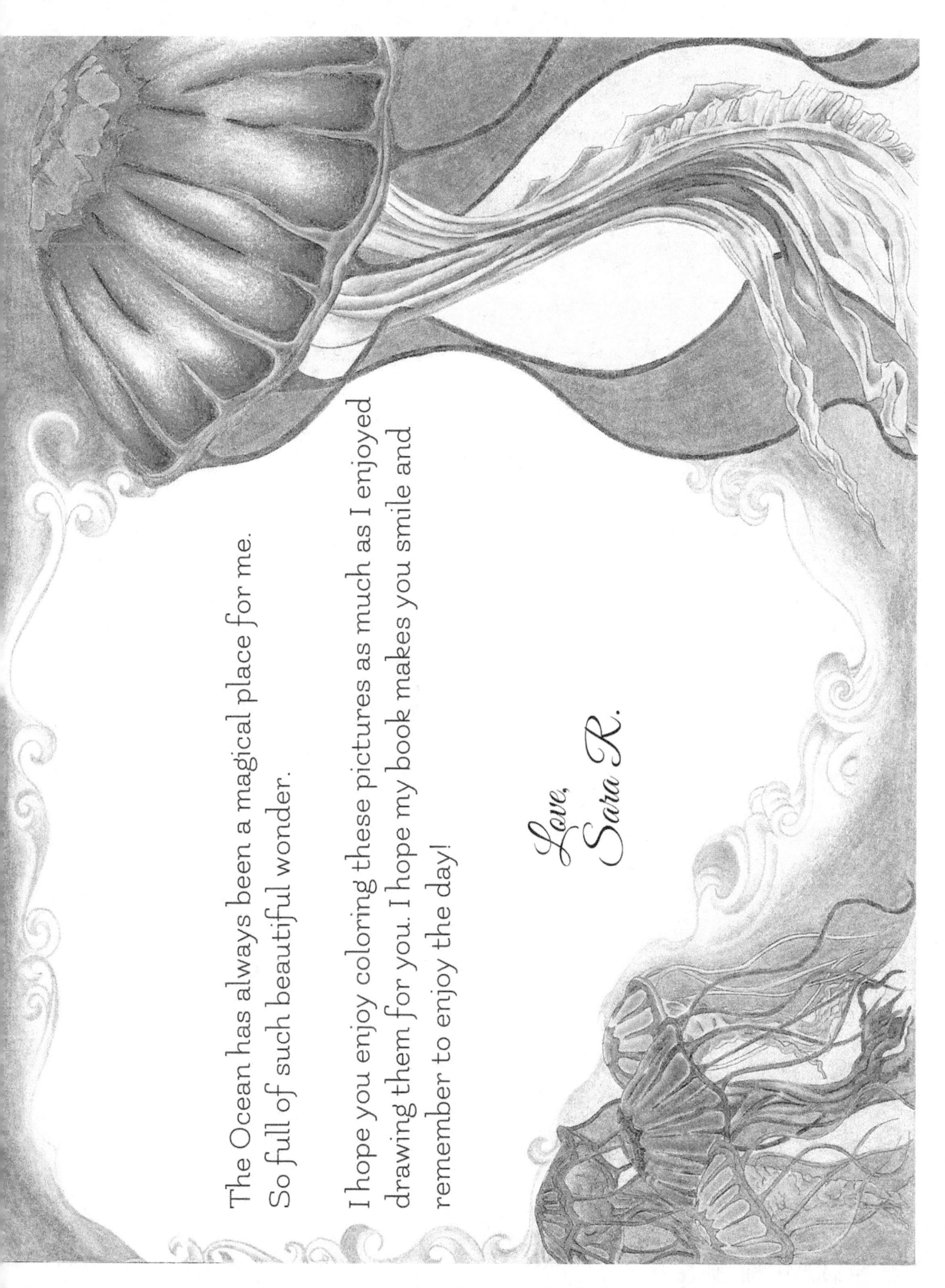

The Ocean has always been a magical place for me.
So full of such beautiful wonder.

I hope you enjoy coloring these pictures as much as I enjoyed
drawing them for you. I hope my book makes you smile and
remember to enjoy the day!

Love,
Sara R.